THE REFERENCE SHELF

Vol. 27   No. 4

REPRESENTATIVE AMERICAN SPEECHES: 1954-1955

Edited, and with Introductions,

by

A. CRAIG BAIRD

Department of Speech, State University of Iowa

THE H. W. WILSON COMPANY

NEW YORK   1955

PREFATORY NOTE

REPRESENTATIVE AMERICAN SPEECHES: 1954-55 is the eighteenth in this annual series. Each volume contains some twenty "representative" speeches by Americans, or by others who have talked in this country (for addresses by Winston Churchill, see earlier volumes). These eighteen volumes include almost 400 addresses by some 270 orators. (See Cumulative Author Index for full list of speakers and their speeches.)

These addresses have been grouped according to subject matter, such as International Policies, National Ideals, Party Politics, Intellectual and Religious Ideals. Students of public address may prefer an alternate classification, based upon the speakers' purposes, speaking occasions, speech types and audiences. The speeches in this volume would be classified somewhat as those given before Congress (Knowland, Stennis, Bricker), political gatherings (Eisenhower, Douglas, Nixon, Stevenson), professional meetings (Dulles, Randall, Lodge, Lippmann), university commencements (Murrow), learned societies (Brebner), community groups (MacArthur), television audiences (Dulles, Peale), religious assemblies (Oxnam, Peale).

The editor, as he has previously stated, makes no claim that the speeches are the "best" of the thousands delivered during these twelve months. He assumes that these speakers delivered remarks that had more than passing significance—through the weight of their ideas, or delivery, or through some combination of these speaking factors. He assumes that speechmaking is to be estimated in terms of audience response, and that the large company of speakers in these eighteen volumes has influenced to some extent the social and other trends of the times.

The Introduction to each of the eighteen volumes deals with some phase of the problem and method of evaluating speeches and speechmakers. The present Introduction attempts to summarize some important economic, political, social, and religious

movements of the day and the relation of the speeches to these events and trends. One way to study the American attitudes and mind, we believe, is to examine the contemporary speech-making in its social setting.

The brief introduction to each address gives the background and usually a brief reference to the speaker, occasion, and the speech itself. The student, in his turn, will delve further into the problems of textual authenticity, immediate speaking situation, thought, supporting materials, structure, emotional and personal appeals, language, delivery, and the immediate and larger effects of the presentation.

The biographical notes in the Appendix will also encourage the reader to explore much further the speaker's background, speech development, and experiences that partly account for the nature and effectiveness of his public speaking.

The Table of Contents of each edition and the Cumulative Author Index at the end of this volume are further aids to a systematic review of speakers and issues since 1937. From the Index the investigator may well compile a list of speakers in any one category (for example, preachers) that would represent a fairly satisfactory list of representatives (since 1937) in that group. (No one volume with its twenty or so speeches can reflect a carefully balanced representation of the various political, economic, religious, educational and other spokesmen. It is hoped that the combined group of four hundred examples may together provide a comprehensive cross section of the preachers, educators, legislators and other types.)

This volume, like its predecessors, is a reference source, useful for subject information and for speeches and speakers to be studied as types. Each volume, in addition to its use as a library reference, is strongly recommended to students of public speaking, extempore speaking, oral and written communication, discussion and debate, history and criticism of American public address, social science, and history, as well as to teachers of such subjects.

The editor is grateful to the various speakers and publishers for their cooperation in providing authentic texts and in giving permission for these reprints. Special acknowledgment is made in each case. The editor appreciates the cooperation of the university libraries and staffs, especially of Dr. Ralph Ellsworth, Director of Libraries, State University of Iowa and his staff; and of John Sykes Hartin, Director of Libraries, University of Mississippi, and his staff.

A. CRAIG BAIRD

June 1, 1955

CONTENTS

RELIGION

INTRODUCTION

Every speaker is heavily affected by the political, economic, and cultural climate in which he lives and speaks. The times make the orator. As Ralph Waldo Emerson remarked, "Times of eloquence are times of terror." Whether on occasion he creates and popularizes the cause about which he is eloquent is of course debatable. In any case, the impact of history is strong. The ebb and flow of historical change, the energy of the movements, no doubt strongly influence many to speak out with high emotion as well as with logical conviction and method. Others, I admit, remain silent under the pressures. The student of speeches, then, will not only be interested in the biography of his speaker, but will also note the cultural history of the times. He will inquire concerning the issues and trends that called forth speakers and stimulated thousands of others to listen and in many cases to follow.

The present period and immediate year of 1954-55, "The Hydrogen Age," is marked by complex patterns of political and social change. The student, through his alertness to these social settings, will more properly have insight into the purposes, content, and mood of a given address. Only by understanding of such context, only by a sensitiveness to the passions of these hours and the behavior of the American people can we best understand the document itself.

What are some of the major problems, and the accompanying attitudes and activities of our population, that find close parallel in the trends and character of the speechmaking of the preceding twelve months? [1]

INTERNATIONAL PROBLEMS

Indo-China

With Korea settled in an armed truce, with no political or other settlements in prospect, the center of the Far East military storm shifted to Indo-China. The French defense, in the eighth

[1] For comparison see *Representative American Speeches: 1953-54*, "Introduction," p9-17.

year of the Viet-Namese war, definitely deteriorated. The Communist capture of Dienbienphu climaxed the French military tragedy. The scene then moved to Geneva and to the negotiations that ended on June 13, 1954, in the partition of Viet-Nam—the North to the Communists, the South to the free peoples. Mendès-France, the new French premier, bore the responsibility for this French "surrender."

These events of mid-1954 stirred prolonged debate up and down the United States. Should the United States transfer its military might and activity from Korea to Indo-China? Should it rescue the crumbling front against this stepped-up Communist aggression? What of our policy, announced earlier by Secretary of State Dulles, of "massive retaliation"? Should we attempt to line up militarily the Western European nations against these Red China moves? (Europe was unsympathetic to such a suggestion, as were most Americans.) Should the United States share in these Geneva armistice talks? (We decided otherwise.) Should we effect a military pact with other Far Eastern nations to resist further inroads? (Secretary Dulles engineered such a treaty, signed at Manila on September 8, 1954.)

Senators Joseph Kennedy and William Knowland, for example, held forth in the Senate against each other on April 6, 1954, on the policy to be followed in the Indo-China struggle. Congressman Judd periodically denounced Red China, for example on May 19. Henry Cabot Lodge, Jr., United States delegate to the United Nations, continued to argue before that body and elsewhere against the admission of Red China to the United Nations; e.g., in his speeches of March 29, April 19, May 7, June 10, and September 15, 1954.

Formosa

Once the fighting in Indo-China ended, at least temporarily, Peiping stepped up its "vest pocket" war against the small Nationalist-held islands off the China coast. And the Red China government declared with increasing vehemence its determination to capture Formosa itself. The tension mounted when Peiping announced on November 23 the imprisonment of eleven American fliers, alleged spies, captured during the Korean war. The United Nations, 47 to 5, condemned this Chinese act (December 10, 1954). United Nations Secretary Dag Hammarskjold journeyed to the Communist Chinese capital (January 1955) to attempt the release of these prisoners. We had already (December 2, 1954) ratified a treaty pledging our defense of Formosa and the Pescadores and of "such other islands as may be determined."

In January 1955, the Communists captured Yikiang, Nationalist held island, and on January 24 the Senate and House approved almost unanimously President Eisenhower's request to use the American forces to defend Formosa and the neighboring islands.

The Security Council of the United Nations at the end of January requested that China enter into a parley looking to a cease fire in the Formosan area. China refused. With the Seventh fleet and air forces standing by, the United States evacuated all troops and civilians from Tachen Island to Taipei, without interference from Red China, February 11. The supreme danger spots shifted to the islands further south, especially the Matsus and Quemoy.

These successive events all provoked strong debate within Congress and without. What was China up to? Did she seek war? Should the United States proceed with an ultimatum to free its imprisoned fliers? (We decided otherwise.) Were we ready to risk a third world war (on the assumption that Russia would give full support to Red China)? Should we abandon defense islands other than Formosa and the Pescadores? Should we agree to give to the United Nations the decision as to the legal future of Formosa? Should we abandon our support of Chiang Kai-shek and thus pave the way for the capture of the island by the Reds? Should we support the entrance of Red China into the United Nations? Secretary Dulles, again, was in the thick of the argument, with explanations to Congress and to the public (e.g., his address of February 16, 1955). Senators debated these issues on the floor of the Senate, including Mansfield (January 24, 1955), Knowland, (January 26), Smith of New Jersey, Lehman, and Morse (January 27), Capehart (January 28), and George (February 1).

Radio and television commentators and a long list of government officials and prominent political and professional leaders battled over the problem. The colleges and universities also argued for their national question whether the United States should recognize Red China.

Western Europe

During 1944-55 the main stream of the cold war continued to center in Europe. The main issue was: Why, when, and how should Germany be rearmed and brought within the European Defense Community? The situation suddenly became ominous when Premier Mendès-France presented the Western European treaty for a vote by the French National Assembly and there allowed it to be killed on August 30, 1954. The French still feared a revived Germany. The French Premier swiftly moved to place the arming of Germany under control of the North Atlantic Alliance. Sir Anthony Eden, in a historic commitment, pledged British troops on the continent and thus paved the way for a new pact on German rearmament. Konrad Adenauer, of West Germany, in effect agreed not to press German demands for control of the Saar. On October 22, the Western Powers concluded the Paris pacts admitting a rearmed West Germany to the North Atlantic alliance. Russia warned the West that if the Paris pacts were ratified, nothing would remain to be negotiated. In December she stepped up her violent propaganda. At the end of 1954 the French Assembly nevertheless voted for the West Germany rearmament.

Malenkov suddenly resigned, on February 8, 1955, with the elevation of a new Soviet regime, including Bulganin, the new premier, and Zhukov and Khrushchev. The startled world attempted to adjust its policies and thinking to this major turnover inside Russia. The overthrow of Mendès-France on February 5 did not help the Western cause at that juncture.

In the United States, public and private speech asked during these critical months, Did the Malenkov regime that talked dramatically of coexistence and played up everywhere the dove of peace really want peace? Was the Russian possession of the hydrogen bomb a prelude to a sudden Pearl Harbor that would destroy overnight Western resistance? Was France a decadent nation no longer to be counted on for "Big Three" leadership? Was the Acheson-Dulles-Truman-Eisenhower policy in Europe getting us nowhere and only creating more American enemies among our allies? Was our propaganda failing? Should we have a try at negotiations with the top Kremlinites? Would the rearming of Germany lead to a deal between that nation and Moscow?

Right- and left-wing Republicans debated sharply against each other on the wisdom of the Eisenhower-Dulles words and moves. Spokesman for militancy was Senator Knowland. On July 1, 1954, he declared to the Senate that if Red China were voted into the United Nations, he would demand that the United States withdraw from that agency. On November 15 he attacked the policy of so-called coexistence of the Communists and the Free Nations. President Eisenhower, however, continued to speak temperately and to calm the indignation that stirred this nation. With our planes shot down off Korea, our airmen imprisoned, and our nation repeatedly bombarded with onslaughts from Moscow (e.g., Molotov's two-and-one-half-hour barrage against us before the Supreme Soviet on February 8, 1955), Americans were demanding some sort of retaliation. Secretary Dulles, between his flights to the East, to England and Europe, continued to report the direction and intent of America's foreign policy. His address of November 29 was a comprehensive view of the situation; [2] that of February 16, 1955, pleaded for peace and a "cease fire" in the Formosan region. His aim was to conciliate both Chiang Kai-shek and the British government in our Formosan military decisions.

[2] See below, p 19-29.

Control of Atoms and Disarmament

Behind these arguments concerning specific American moves in Europe and Asia was the ever more crucial problem of what to do about hydrogen-atom weapons and disarmament. General of the Army Douglas MacArthur, at Los Angeles, on January 26, 1955,[3] called for consolidated world opinion in support of disarmament. The United Nations continued to discuss the issue. It was the agency to which many looked for any progress in cooperative disarmament.

DOMESTIC PROBLEMS

Communism and Censure of Senator McCarthy

Communism in the United States continued not only as a military and ideological menace, but as a politically dramatic issue. Senator Joseph McCarthy became the center of a six months' violent investigation. Were his techniques undermining Army and civilian morale? Did they bring disrepute on the Senate itself? The Senator's committee, the Senate Permanent Investigations Subcommittee, set to work under the temporary chairmanship of Senator Karl Mundt of South Dakota to determine the facts in dispute. Did Senator McCarthy and his chief counsel, Roy Cohn, try to get favored treatment for Private David Schine? Did the Army try to stop Senator McCarthy's investigation of security risks at Fort Monmouth? Did the Army use Schine as a "hostage"? The nation, via radio and television, watched and listened to the details of the thirty-six days' investigation. The results were that a majority (four Republicans, Senators Mundt, Dirksen, Dworshak, and Potter) mildly criticized Senator McCarthy. The minority report of Democratic Senators McClellan, Symington, and Jackson was more severe.

The Senate, before adjourning in August, set up a bipartisan committee of six to report to the Senate later on the charges of

[3] See below, p34-42.

censure of Senator McCarthy. The Senate reconvened on November 8 and officially on December 2, 67 to 22, "condemned" the Wisconsin Senator. This entire affair, over these many months, not only produced prolonged and acrimonious speaking in the Senate and endless wrangling in the investigating bodies themselves, but stimulated endless arguments over the land. Almost everyone, it seemed, was either violently pro- or anti-McCarthy.[4]

Political Campaign

The election of November 2, 1954, gave the Eighty-fourth Congress, both the House and Senate, to the Democrats. It also added eight Democratic governors and removed none.

The campaign began apathetically but finished in wild party excitement—at least to the party workers. Never before in a mid-term election had there been so much speaking, so much organization of listeners, and especially so much radio and television coverage. In the final stages the congressional and gubernatorial candidates got down to violent personalities. The New York *Times* called the campaign a violation of "decency, honesty, and fair play."

The issues, aside from the local cross currents, were: Was the Democratic party soft on communism? Were the Republicans responsible for the 3 million unemployed? Should the voters endorse the Republican flexible farm price supports? What of the Republican sponsored Dixon-Yates contract that injected private power into the TVA program? Should the voters return a Republican congress so as to support President Eisenhower?

The campaign was especially heated in New Jersey (Republican Case the winner), Oregon (Democrat Neuberger, winner), New York (gubernatorial candidates Harriman vs. Ives), Wyoming (Democrat O'Mahoney the winner) and Illinois (Democrat Paul Douglas the winner).[5] Adlai E. Stevenson entered the speaking early and maintained his reputation for

[4] See below Senator Bricker's speech, p 113-22; and Senator Stennis's speech, p 109-12.

[5] For Senator Douglas's speech of September 25, see below, p81-8.

effective stump and television [6] campaigning. Vice President Nixon also spoke unceasingly and covered most of the Northern pivotal states.[7] President Eisenhower campaigned more vigorously than any previous President in a mid-term election. Especially did he attempt a "rescue" series of appeals during the final two weeks.[8]

All in all the quantity and dramatic aggressiveness (but not the quality) of the political speechmaking exceeded those of any previous mid-term campaign.

Foreign Trade

The perennial problem of our foreign economic policy came dramatically to the front early in 1955. The previous Congress had reluctantly renewed for one year the Reciprocal Trade Agreement Act, but the Democratic Congress, January 1955, immediately called for the extension of the act for three more years. Again the debate became nation-wide. The tariff issue was the national debate question for the high schools during the 1954-55 season.[9]

Education

The Supreme Court's unanimous decision that segregation of whites and Negroes in public schools was unconstitutional set off a vigorous chain of public speaking, especially in Southern legislatures. Many Southern speakers, in legislatures and out, roundly criticized the Supreme Court and proposed ways and means of evading any edict to end separate but equal education.

School and college educators also concerned themselves with the recurrent issues: What is liberal education? Are the humanities and liberal training to succumb more and more to

[6] For Mr. Stevenson's speech of October 30, see below, p99-108.
[7] For Mr. Nixon's speech of November 1, see below, p89-98.
[8] For President Eisenhower's address of October 8, see below, p71-80.
[9] For speech by Clarence B. Randall, "Our Foreign Economic Policy," December 14, 1954, see below, p55-69.

professionalism? And is education to resist the trend toward political and other conformity? [10] Is education in the public schools progressively deteriorating through inadequate teaching staffs and equipment? [11]

Notable was Columbia University's year-long (1953-54) observation of its Bicentennial Anniversary. Many addresses and three formal convocations were held on the general theme of man's right to knowledge and the free use thereof.[12]

Higher educational institutions throughout America, in line with this Columbia University theme, continued to discuss their attitude toward left-wing and communistic teachers and the role of higher institutions in a free industrialized society.

Religion

Finally, preachers and other moral leaders continued to ask, Does the increase in American church membership indicate an increase in genuine religion? Are Americans losing their sense of moral and ethical responsibility? Evangelistic preaching, for example, under Billy Graham, took on a new if temporary vigor. The radio and television preachers continued to have wide prominence and support.[13]

Notable was the two-week World Conference of Churches, at Evanston, Illinois, in August 1954. Some 1500 delegates representing 163 denominations there pondered over ways and means of further uniting the Christian churches.[14]

Thus by radio and expanding television, wherever Americans, young or old, met one another, officially or informally, these events and issues were orally interpreted or argued. Public opinion developed, and American life, always changing, took on a recognizable character.

[10] Edward R. Murrow, "Commencement Address," June 6, 1954, p 128-33.

[11] Walter Lippmann, "Educational Deficit and National Crisis," March 19, 1954, p 134-44.

[12] J. B. Brebner, "Common Ground of Humility," October 31, 1954, p 123-7.

[13] Norman Vincent Peale, "How to Have Good Relations with Other People," October 18, 1953, p 153-60.

[14] G. Bromley Oxnam, "We Intend to Stay Together," August 15, 1954, p 145-52; Robert L. Calhoun, "Christ—The Hope of the World," August 15, 1954, p 161-73.

FOREIGN RELATIONS

GOAL OF OUR FOREIGN POLICY [1]

JOHN FOSTER DULLES [2]

John Foster Dulles, Secretary of State, gave this address at the annual Thomas E. Wilson dinner of the 4-H Congress at the Conrad Hilton Hotel, Chicago, on the evening of November 29, 1954. The audience was made up of 1250 farm youths from all states and territories of the United States, attending the thirty-third annual Congress. They represented two million farm boys and girls, between the ages of ten twenty-one years.

One hour after the delivery of this speech before this visible audience, Secretary Dulles repeated it over the nation-wide radio and television outlets.

Several drafts had been prepared and discarded (according to J. H. Johnson, New York *Times,* Tuesday, November 30, 1954). A State Department attaché reported that Mr. Dulles and his aides had completed the final speech at Watertown, New York, just before taking a plane for Chicago that day.

Mr. Dulles believes in the importance of effective communication— both to his high level governmental associates and to the rank and file of the citizenry. He works hard to make unmistakably clear his policies and ideas. When he finds that he has been misunderstood he tries again, "tirelessly editing his own public speeches and even his thoughts." He believes that the millions of his countrymen are entitled to know his business and are capable of doing so—if the addresses are properly composed.

Although no orator, he has repeatedly demonstrated clear expression, as illustrated by his televised extempore report to the Cabinet (and to the nation) of the Paris Conference, from which he had returned a few hours previously. The Chicago speech illustrated his satisfactory adjustment to these younger Americans (as well as to the general radio-television listeners and viewers).

Significant at Chicago was his emphasis on the aim of the United States to use every method to maintain peace. (He had been accused not only by the Communists but by some leaders of the free nations of "warmongering.")

[1] Text supplied by the State Department.
[2] For biographical note, see Appendix.

Secretary Dulles was hailed as the "Man of the Year" in foreign relations. He had journeyed more than 100,000 miles during 1954 in his conferences in South America, Japan, Formosa, and Manila, and in his repeated conferences in Europe. He was given considerable credit for helping settle the troubled situations in Egyptian conflicts with Britain over the Suez; the Iran decision to allow resumption by foreign firms of the oil industry; the treaty between Turkey and Pakistan; the Latin American states' agreement to fight any Communist aggression in this hemisphere; the rescue of Guatemala from Communist seizure; and the steps to set up the Western European defense system, including the proposed rearming of Germany with the approval of Mendès-France's French government. But the victory of the Chinese Communists in Southeast Asia and their further drives were ominous. Our State Department and the Administration were still challenged by the major China-Korea-Formosa-Indo-China problem to be dealt with in 1955.[3]

Ten days ago at the White House I discussed our foreign policy with the congressional leaders of both parties, Republicans and Democrats. Afterwards, the President told me he thought it would be a good idea for me to report also to the American people.

It is not easy to compress the whole story into a short talk. But I shall do my best.

Let me begin by emphasizing the goal of our foreign policy —it is to enable you and me and our children to enjoy in peace the blessings of liberty. That purpose is back of everything we do.

The task is not an easy one, for international communism threatens both peace and liberty, by many means, at many places.

One ever-present danger is the danger of being fooled into dropping our guard before the peril is really past.

The international Communists are masters at the trick of using words which mean one thing to them and another thing to us.

It took us time to learn that the word "democracy" means, to Communists, a dictatorship—what they call "dictatorship of the proletariat."

[3] For further comment on John Foster Dulles as speaker, see *Representative American Speeches: 1947-48*, p58-67; *1948-49*, p207-15; *1949-50*, p15-27; *1950-51*, p54-64; *1951-52*, p41-7; *1952-53*, p 15-20; *1953-54*, p33-43.

It took us time to learn that the word "peace" means, to international Communists, a world of conformity—conformity with a pattern of conduct prescribed by Moscow.

Now the trick word is "coexistence." To us it means tolerance of differences. It remains to be seen what it means to international Communists. It is true that the Russian Communists have recently talked more softly. But it is equally true that the Chinese Communists have talked and acted with increasing violence. They break their armistice agreements and they outrage the elemental decencies of international conduct.

Perhaps international communism is trying by a new way to divide the free nations. They seek to be soothing in Europe. They are provocative in Asia.

Our nation will react, and react vigorously, to the outrages against our citizens, but without allowing ourselves to be intemperately provoked into action which would be a violation of our international obligations and which would impair the alliance of the free nations. What has happened is a challenge to us, and indeed to all who want peace, to find ways, consistent with peace, to sustain international rights.

We have agreed, by the United Nations Charter, to try to settle international disputes by peaceful means in such a manner that international peace is not endangered. Therefore our first duty is to exhaust peaceful means of sustaining our international rights and those of our citizens, rather than now resorting to war action such as a naval and air blockade of Red China.

Of course, we look anxiously for signs of real change in the attitude of international Communists. We hope that the day will come when they will renounce the effort to rule the world by methods of force, intimidation, and fraud. When that new day dawns we shall greet it eagerly. But we want to be sure that we do not mistake a false dawn for the real dawn.

There is still a vast Russian military establishment, far in excess of any defensive needs. The Chinese Communists are still aggressive. There is still, in every free country, a Communist apparatus seeking to overthrow the established order.

Therefore, we must remain vigilant. We must have policies to meet both the military risk and the subversive risk, and we do have such policies.

There are some people in the United States, and there are more in other lands, who contend that it is wrong to be ready and able to fight. They say that the true peace-lovers should be unarmed and neutral.

We have tried that, and it did not work.

We were unarmed and neutral in 1914 when the First World War came. The aggressors felt that they could count us out.

We were unarmed and neutral in 1939 when the Second World War came. Again the aggressors thought they could count us out.

The Korean War came after we had largely disarmed and withdrawn our troops from Korea, and the aggressors thought that they would be unopposed.

Today we take a different view. We believe that the greatest contribution we can make to peace is to be ready to fight, if need be, and to have the resources and the allies to assure that an aggressor would surely be defeated. That does not mean being truculent or provocative or militaristic. It does mean seeking peace not only with the heart, but also with the mind.

In that mood, we make military preparations which, we believe, will deter war. That requires, basically, that a potential aggressor shall not think that aggression is a paying proposition. He must know that he cannot destroy the United States by sudden attack and that we have the capacity to counterattack.

So, we are developing continental defense in a major way. It will consist of an elaborate series of early warning systems and interceptors which apply the latest scientific knowledge. These should enable us to knock down a very high percentage of any Red bombers engaged in hostile missions against the United States.

Then, we have our Strategic Air Command which is capable of delivering retaliatory blows against vital parts of the Soviet Union. These blows, we calculate, would do damage far in excess of that which Red planes could inflict upon the United States.

You may ask what foreign policy has to do with this. My answer is: everything. Our continental defense system depends on Canada. And the free nations cannot have effective retaliatory power to deter aggression without air fields in widely scattered places.

Therefore, a vital part of our foreign policy is to have friendly relations with many other countries so that we can work together for our common defense.

I can report that we *do* have such friendly relations and that, as a result, we can make it unprofitable for any nation to attack the United States.

Of course, we could not have that relationship if we thought only of ourselves. The relationship must be for the common good. So, the common defense includes many areas outside the United States.

It is particularly important that the great oceans should be dominated by free and friendly nations. We have made this clear by a series of security treaties. The Atlantic area is covered by the North Atlantic security treaty. The Pacific area is covered by a series of treaties, some still in process of consummation, which cover Japan, the Republic of Korea, the Ryukyus (Okinawa), Formosa, the Philippines, Australia and New Zealand, and parts of Southeast Asia.

To back up these treaty words there are local forces. In some cases the local forces which seem necessary are larger than the local governments can support. If so, we help out. That, however, is not a "handout." It is something called "foreign aid," although I dislike that phrase. The correct and better phrase is "mutual security."

Western Europe, with its vast industrial power, is a prize of first order to any who seek domination. So it requires special protection. It gets it by NATO. But NATO needs, at its core on the Continent, a greater measure of unity, with German participation. That was the purpose of the historic agreements made last month at London and Paris. These agreements should end the constant warring of European nations against themselves, and at the same time provide Western Europe with effective defense. The prospect of European unity is reinforced by the recent Trieste settlement between Italy and Yugoslavia and the prospective Saar settlement between France and Germany.

In addition to local defense within treaty areas, there is striking power by air or sea. Such mobile forces are needed to deter attack because an aggressor would have a great advantage if he could attack a single locality with assurance of safety against retaliation. We must have the capacity to respond at places and by means of *our* choosing.

This, however, does not mean that any local war would automatically be turned into a general war with atomic bombs being dropped all over the map. The essential thing is that we and our allies should have the means and the will to assure that a potential aggressor would lose from his aggression more than he could win. This does not mean that the aggressor had to be totally destroyed. It does mean a capacity to inflict punishing damage. We believe that we and our allies have the power to do that. We also believe that, so long as we do have that power, it is unlikely that there will be armed attack upon the areas covered by our security arrangements.

There are some areas in the world which are not covered by special collective security arrangements. That is notably the case with reference to portions of Asia.

However, there are trends toward collective security in this area. For example, Turkey and Pakistan have started to create a northern tier of defense which would block off the rich oil fields of the Middle East from easy seizure by the Soviet Union. The recent liberation of Iran from the grip of the Communist Tudeh party, the subsequent oil settlement, and the settlement of the Suez base controversy all open up new possibilities of strength in this part of the world.

In all cases the United Nations provides an overriding shield against open aggression. This is not negligible—as Korea showed. And it is our policy to support vigorously the United Nations.

In the various ways I have outlined, the free nations are largely protected against the danger of armed attack.

The peoples of the world seem to sense this fact. That is why it is now generally felt that there is less danger of world war than seemed to be the case a few years ago.

Let me turn now to the danger which comes from subversion. This danger is great. International communism has had great experience in fomenting political disorder. These successes are not merely measured by governments actually taken over—nearly a score—but by divisions and obstructions which Communists promote within the free world.

A first concern to us in this connection is the situation in the American Republics. The Latin American countries are in no great danger from open armed attack, but they are vulnerable to Communist subversion. We dealt with this matter at the conference which the American nations held at Caracas last March. They there adopted a Declaration to the effect that it would be dangerous to the peace and security of all of the American nations if international communism should gain control of the political institutions of any one of them.

That was a momentous declaration. It may serve the needs of our time as effectively as the Monroe Doctrine served the needs of our nation during the last century. It made clear that collective action to eradicate international communism is not an act of intervention, but an act to uproot intervention.

The principle of this Caracas Declaration had a special bearing on the situation in Guatemala. There international communism had in fact got control of the Government. The American States were about to meet with reference to this danger when the Guatemalan people themselves backed loyal elements who cut out the cancer of communism. The Communist-directed President of Guatemala ignominiously fled, and the leader of the liberation movement is now the President of Guatemala.

This Caracas Declaration, and the demonstration that the American States take it seriously, greatly protect this hemisphere against Communist subversion. The Communists know that if they should get control of the political institutions of an American State they can expect the other American States to be

against them. Therefore, there is less incentive to seek control than has been the case heretofore.

The American nations are also trying to achieve sounder economies. There is now taking place at Rio an economic conference. We hope and believe that this conference will stimulate sound measures to develop the economies and lift up living conditions. It will give practical meaning to President Eisenhower's "good partner" policy.

In Asia and Africa the dangers of subversion are great. In these continents there are countries without self-government, many of their political institutions are not yet firmly rooted, the economies are weak, and the governments often are insecure. The situation in Viet-Nam is particularly precarious today, and in North Africa the situation is troubled.

Some of the Asian nations which have recently won independence need help. But they are afraid to take it from the West because they fear that means a rebirth of Western colonialism. So they remain exposed to a brand of communism which breeds the most ruthless colonialists in history.

It must be made clear that the Asian and Western nations can work together as equals. We took a big step in that direction at the Manila Conference of last September. There, both Western and Asian participants joined in a "Pacific Charter," which proclaimed their dedication to the independence and self-government of all peoples everywhere, able to discharge those responsibilities.

That was an important step toward laying the ghost of Western colonialism which still so frightens some free Asian countries that they hesitate to accept helpful association with the West.

There is also need for economic policies which will help to develop all underdeveloped countries. In the Communist countries developments are achieved through a system of forced labor akin to slavery. Living standards are kept very low, and the people are forced to work very hard. In this way heavy industry is developed. It is a cruel system and is primarily for war purposes. It does, however, have a certain fascination for the peoples of undeveloped countries who feel that their own economies are standing still.

In a free society it is normal that the developed countries lend money to the underdeveloped countries. Our United States, in its early days, was partially developed by European capital. Today it is the United States which has the most capital available to help other countries. We must find a way to put it to work. This is good business, for provident loans are usually repaid, and experience shows that we all profit from an environment of prosperity.

I should mention in this connection President Eisenhower's plan for putting atomic energy to peacetime purposes. This plan, when announced at the United Nations last December, stirred a tremendous response. For nearly a year we tried to get the Russians to contribute to the plan. I personally discussed it several times with Mr. Molotov. However, they refused. Then this fall we said we would go ahead with others, leaving the Russians out. Now it seems that, after all, they want to come along.

By this Eisenhower plan our nation reappears in its historic role. We have discovered new possibilities for human welfare and are putting our knowledge at the peaceful service of all mankind.

There is one final aspect of our policies to which I would allude. We believe, as Abraham Lincoln said, that our Declaration of Independence promises "liberty, not alone to the people of this country, but hope for the world for all future time."

Today a third of the human race is in fearful bondage to Communist dictatorships. But we do not regard that as immutable.

There is, we know, vast human discontent among the 800 million people whom international communism rules. That comes from the enslavement of labor, the suppression of religion and of individual initiative, and the national humiliation of the satellite countries.

Liberation normally comes from within. But it is more apt to come from within if hope is constantly sustained from without. That we are doing in many ways.

A significant recent development has been the Soviet change of policy toward Yugoslavia. In 1948 Yugoslavia broke free from the grip of international communism and reasserted its own nationalism.

Until recently, the Yugoslav Government and nation were threatened and reviled by the international Communists of neighboring Hungary, Rumania, and Bulgaria. Now, however, the Soviet Union treats Yugoslavia with deference while it continues to treat with contempt the puppet governments of Hungary, Rumania, and Bulgaria. That may embolden the satellites to demand a measure of independence.

Developments clearly portend the change, at some time, of the absolute rule which international communism asserts over the once free nations of Europe and Asia.

Our policies do not exclude international conferences, even with those who are hostile to us. In that way we ended the Korean War. The scope of conferences with the Soviet Government is necessarily limited by our attitude toward the captive peoples, for the Soviets know that we will not make any deal which would condone and perpetuate the captivity of men and nations.

Also, we do not want to talk with the Soviet representatives when their only purpose is to divide the free nations and prevent their taking necessary measures for their own security.

We had one such meeting at Berlin last January and February. The ostensible purpose was to unify Germany and to liberate Austria. In fact, the Soviet Foreign Minister only sought to block the plans for Western European security.

We do want to find out whether the Soviet Union will sign the Austrian Treaty and whether, after the London and Paris accords are ratified, it will talk seriously about uniting Germany. That is the purpose of a note we delivered to the Soviet Government today.

We are also, of course, deeply interested in the limitation of armaments. A principal purpose of the London-Paris accords is not merely to create defensive strength in Western Europe but to limit and control that strength so that it can never be an aggressive force. There opened today at Moscow a so-called "security conference" where the Soviet leaders will talk to their puppets and they in turn will respond as ordered. We shall see whether the Soviet Union takes this occasion to match the West by imposing reasonable limits on military establishments in that part of Europe which it controls.

There is often a tendency on the part of free peoples to see their own faults and weaknesses and to exaggerate the strength and successes of others. Of course, we should subject ourselves to constant self-criticism. That is the way to betterment.

We need not, however, feel that we are now failing in the great struggle which has been forced upon us. We are entitled to be confident because we are strong in ourselves and strong in the good partnership we have with our allies.

The reality of the matter is that the United States, by every standard of measurement, is the world's greatest power not only materially but spiritually. We have national policies which are clear and sound. They fit a civilization based on religious faith. They are strongly implemented, but at a cost we can afford to live with. They have evolved on a nonpartisan basis and, in broad outline, they are overwhelmingly backed by our people. Such policies, I am supremely confident, will peacefully prevail.

COEXISTENCE AND ATOMIC STALEMATE [4]

WILLIAM F. KNOWLAND [5]

Senator William F. Knowland, Republican of California, majority leader of the Senate, gave this address in the Senate, on November 15, 1954, on the problem of "coexistence" of the United States and Soviet Russia. His argument, extending over several hours and interrupting debate on the censure of Senator McCarthy, was a vigorous attack upon the Administration's foreign policy. He argued in effect that either Eisenhower's policy should be officially endorsed by the Senate, or that a "basic change" be made in that policy.

President Eisenhower had been following a moderate line. Even after the Communists had shot down an American plane off the coast of Japan a few days before, the President told the press that Russia seemed to be adopting a more conciliatory policy. Earlier the President had vetoed a proposal by three members of the Joint Chiefs of Staff, Admirals Arthur Radford and Robert Carney, and General Nathan Twining, Air Force Chief of Staff, that the Chinese Nationalists be permitted to bomb inland China to prevent a Communist landing on the Nationalist island of Quemoy.

Senator Knowland's theme was that time was not necessarily on our side in this "peaceful coexistence"; that something must be done other than what seemed to be done; and that Congress should review the cold war and help to shape a clear-cut policy. The issue was, Could the free and Communist worlds exist permanently side by side without all-out war? Knowland replied negatively.

As he spoke the Russians were stormily protesting against any Paris agreement to a Western Defense program. French Premier Mendès-France had flown to Washington to confer on the problem.

President Eisenhower the next day expressed full confidence in the policy of Secretary of State Dulles. And the Secretary himself said that he saw no "immediate emergency" that would warrant "unusual examination" of our foreign policy. Part of the issue between the Eisenhower and the Knowland divisions of the Republican party lay in the meaning of "peaceful coexistence." Dulles suggested that "modus vivendi" would be a more appropriate term.

Senator Knowland, whose political opponents refer to him as "the Senator from Formosa," had long advocated a radical military and political policy in dealing with Red China. On July 1, 1954, for example, he had addressed the Senate on the subject and announced: "On the day

[4] *Congressional Record.* 100:14903-10. November 15, 1954 (daily edition).
[5] For biographical note, see Appendix.

when Communist China is voted into membership into the United Nations, I shall resign my majority leadership in the Senate . . . so that I can devote my full efforts in the Senate and throughout the country in terminating United States membership in that organization. . . ." A persistent debater and a speaker of power, he commanded substantial support in the Republican right wing. In 1955 further Senate debate on foreign policy seemed to be in the offing with the Executive split and with Senator Knowland leading the Senate opposition against a moderate stand toward Russia and Red China.

Mr. President, recent developments abroad and at home justify, in my mind, interrupting the debate on the pending resolution. At an early date I shall discuss the pending resolution and modifications of it.

Grave problems and dangers confront our Republic, and they are of far greater importance than the pending business before the Senate. We must keep matters in their proper perspective.

Are "coexistence" and "atomic stalemate" synonymous terms? If they are not, just what is the difference? Is the former merely an inevitable prelude to the latter? And what of our foreign policy and our defense policy when such an atomic stalemate takes place? Does not atomic stalemate mean inevitable Communist nibbling aggression, rather than peace in our time? How many years remain when we still have some initiative left? These are some of the basic questions before the Government and the people of the United States.

Certainly they are so important and the results of the decisions made are so far-reaching that the Congress and the American people must be taken into the confidence of the administration.

No matter what the decisions are in the elections of 1956, a Republican administration and a Democratic-controlled Congress in the months immediately ahead share a heavy responsibility for the survival of this Republic, and the possibility of a free world of free men hangs in the balance.

The civilizations that flourished and died in the past had opportunities for a limited period of time to change the course of history. Sooner or later, however, they passed "the point of no return," and the decisions were no longer theirs to make.

Coexistence and atomic stalemate will result in ultimate Communist victory. Unless one believes that the men in the Kremlin have completely changed their long-term strategy of ultimately having a Communist world, and no longer follow the doctrine that, in order to achieve their ends, anything is allowable, including deception and treachery, we must face the fact that the Communist concept of peaceful coexistence means that the United States or other free nations of the world will be allowed to exist only until communism is able to subvert them from within or destroy them by aggression from without.

It is my belief that the Soviet Union is advancing the Trojan horse of coexistence only for the purpose of gaining sufficient time to accomplish what we may term "atomic stalemate." When would they hope to accomplish this objective? The target date is probably between 1957 and 1960.

There is some fallacious thinking that when that point arrives the world will have gained a stalemate peace because neither side will then dare to use or threaten to use its atomic power against the other. At that point, so the reasoning runs, the two great world powers, the United States and the Soviet Union, will checkmate and immobilize each other and a sort of troubled peace will settle down over the balance of the world.

Certainly we must face up to the fact that the superiority the United States has today in a stockpile of atomic weapons and the means of delivering them will be checkmated, and the nations which today are toying with neutralism will be actively proclaiming it.

Let us examine the possibility then of even a troubled peace. It is more likely that at that point, when the free world has become paralyzed and immobilized by the realization that the United States and the Soviet Union could act and react one upon the other with overwhelming devastation, that the men in the Kremlin will see their best opportunity to start with what for the want of a better term I will call "operation nibbling," wherein they will seek to take over the peripheral nations bite by bite.

At that point, through the capitals of what remain of our anxious allies and with loud voices from the neutralists, as well as from sources in our own country, will rise the anguished cry, "Should we risk all-out atomic war for Iran, Sweden, Afghanistan, Yugoslavia, India, Finland, Burma, and so forth?" "For after all," the argument will run, "we have no treaty obligations to them." Then they will start down through our smaller allies first to soften us up. These will not all be nibbled at once, but will be spaced out so that as each country passes behind the Iron Curtain, it will increase the despair of the other victims and the paralysis of the nations which might be willing to resist.

Since stalemate would put the Soviet Union itself off limits, the intended victim of the aggression could only look forward to a localized war within their own frontiers with the destruction of life and property that would entail. Since there would be no hope of restraining this new type of Soviet aggression by placing the body of the octopus in danger, these nations individually, one by one, might prefer to accept Soviet terms rather than even call on the West for aid.

Before our eyes the people of the United States would see nation after nation nibbled away and when the realization finally dawned that this policy would inevitably result in our country becoming a continental Dienbienphu in a Communist totalitarian world, the chances of our winning such a struggle would be so lessened and the Soviet world so extended that they then would be prepared for an all-out challenge to us wherein we would be allowed the choice to surrender or die.

It seems to me that the responsible committees of the Congress should promptly summon the State and Defense officials and the Joint Chiefs of Staff to fully inquire into our foreign and defense policy to find out where in their judgment it will take us and whether this clear and present danger which appears to me to exist is such that a basic change in the direction of our policy is warranted.

Time is running out and I would remind the Senate that in this day and age of the airplane and the atomic weapon, time is not necessarily on the side of the free world.

SEVENTY-FIFTH BIRTHDAY ADDRESS [6]

DOUGLAS MACARTHUR [7]

General of the Army Douglas MacArthur celebrated his seventy-fifth birthday on January 26, 1955, with three addresses in Los Angeles. Before an enthusiastic crowd of fifteen thousand in MacArthur Park he spoke briefly at the dedication of a civic monument in his honor. At a luncheon given by the Episcopal Diocese of Los Angeles he acknowledged the receipt of an award of extraordinary merit from the Right Reverend Francis Eric Bloy, Bishop of the Diocese. MacArthur's third address, printed below, given at a civic banquet in his honor that evening, was sponsored by the Los Angeles County Council of the American Legion.

Before the American Legion audience, the General appealed to this nation "to proclaim our readiness to abolish war in concert with the great powers of the world." Said he, "The fate of the Far East will not be settled by force of arms. We may all be practically annihilated—but war can no longer be an arbiter of survival."

The evening address, like the earlier one at the unveiling of the monument, was couched in lofty language. The speaker uttered broad truths; referred to his personal background and sentiments; analyzed the causes of war; touched on the strategy and military outcomes of the Far Eastern war; and gave his own solution: peace through public opinion.

The address was another example of General MacArthur's ability to compose and deliver an oration in the grand style of a former generation. His delivery, consonant with his oral style, was sonorous, emphatic, eloquent.

Adverse critics noted the speaker's by-passing the role of the United Nations in influencing a program of abolishing war through the substitution of an adequate legal system. And meantime President Eisenhower's program of preparedness to avert suicide through sharp conquest by our enemies was not to be dismissed. [8]

Your Excellency, Your Honor, Judge Pfaff, Commander Goshaw, and all those present tonight in this distinguished assemblage:

Seldom in history has living man been honored as this famous community of Los Angeles has honored me today. You

---

[6] Text is from the *Congressional Record*. 101: Appendix 682-3. February 7, 1955 (daily edition). Reprinted here by permission of General of the Army Douglas MacArthur.

[7] For biographical note, see Appendix.

[8] For further comment on General MacArthur as speaker, see *Representative American Speeches: 1945-46.* p 13-15; *1951-52,* p21-30.

have etched in my heart an unforgettable memory of patriotic fervor and national devotion. You have aroused an indelible emotion of gratitude that I am unable to express adequately in words. Yet, the reality of life enables me to apply an appraising perspective; to understand that your action springs not so much from a desire to memorialize a personality as to proclaim a people's adherence to ideals long ago fabricated into the warp and woof of what is called the American way of life. That you have chosen me to symbolize this rich heritage of principles is an honor which makes me feel far greater than any just merit; that my name should stand for the millions of unnamed others whose faith and courage built the immortal way from which was fashioned the true greatness of our country creates within me a feeling of humility far in excess of all possible pride. It makes me revere the stars in our Flag far more than any stars on my shoulders.

I am so grateful to all who have wished me birthday greetings. I know such expressions of good will would have brightened the eyes of that gentle Virginia lady, my mother, on this her day. Thank you—thank you in her name again and again—and, as "Old soldiers never die," I promise to keep on living as though I expected to live forever. That famous barrack room ballad apparently counts on us, those Old Soldiers who have escaped the carnage of the battlefield, to find the Fountain of Youth. And, indeed, we might if we only understood what the poet said, that youth is not entirely a time of life—it is a state of mind. It is not wholly a matter of ripe cheeks, red lips or supple knees. It is a temper of the will, a quality of the imagination, a vigor of the emotions, a freshness of the deep springs of life. It means a temperamental predominance of courage over timidity, of an appetite for adventure over love of ease. Nobody grows old by merely living a number of years. People grow old only by deserting their ideals. Years may wrinkle the skin, but to give up interest wrinkles the soul. Worry, doubt, self-distrust, fear and despair—these are the long, long years that bow the head and turn the growing spirit back to dust. Whatever your years, there is in every being's heart the love of wonder, the undaunted challenge of events, the unfailing child-like appetite for what next, and the joy and the game of life. You are as young as your faith, as old as your doubt; as young as your self-confidence, as old as your fear; as young as your hope, as old as your despair. In the central place of every heart there is a recording chamber; so long as it receives messages of beauty, hope, cheer and courage, so long are you young. When the wires are all down and your heart is covered with the snows of pessimism and the ice of cynicism, then, and then only are you grown old—and then, indeed, as the ballad says, you just fade away.

Many in this brilliant audience were my comrades-in-arms in the days of used-to-be. They have known war in all its horror and, as veterans, hope against its recurrence. How, we ask ourselves, did such an institution become so integrated with man's life and civilization? How has it grown to be the most vital factor in our existence? It started in a modest enough way as a sort of gladiatorial method of settling disputes between conflicting tribes. One of the oldest and most classical examples is the Biblical story of David and Goliath. Each of the two contesting groups selected its champion. They fought and based upon the outcome an agreement resulted. Then, as time went on, small professional groups known as armies replaced the individual champions. And these groups fought in some obscure corner of the world and victory or defeat was accepted as the basis of an ensuing peace. And from then on, down through the ages, the constant record is an increase in the character and strength of the forces with the rate of increase always accelerating. From a small percentage of the populace it finally engulfed all. It is now the nation in arms.

Within the span of my own life I have witnessed this evolution. At the turn of the century, when I entered the Army, the target was one enemy casualty at the end of a rifle or bayonet or sword. Then came the machine gun designed to kill by the dozen. After that, the heavy artillery raining death upon the hundreds. Then the aerial bomb to strike by the thousands— followed by the atom explosion to reach the hundreds of thousands. Now, electronics and other processes of science have raised the destructive potential to encompass millions. And with restless hands we work feverishly in dark laboratories to find the means to destroy all at one blow.

But, this very triumph of scientific annihilation—this very success of invention—has destroyed the possibility of war being a medium of *practical* settlement of international differences. The enormous destruction to both sides of closely matched opponents makes it impossible for the winner to translate it into anything but his own disaster.

The Second World War, even with its now antiquated armaments, clearly demonstrated that the victor had to bear in large part the very injuries inflicted on his foe. Our own country spent billions of dollars and untold energies to heal the wounds of Germany and Japan. War has become a Frankenstein to destroy both sides. No longer is it the weapon of adventure whereby a short cut to international power and wealth—a place in the sun—can be gained. If you lose, you are annihilated. If you win, you stand only to lose. No longer does it possess the chance of the winner of a duel—it contains rather the germs of double suicide. Science has clearly outmoded it as a feasible arbiter. The great question is—does this mean that war can now be outlawed from the world? If so, it would mark the greatest advance in civilization since the Sermon on the Mount. It would lift at one stroke the darkest shadow which has engulfed mankind from the beginning. It would not only remove fear and bring security—it would not only create new moral and spiritual values—it would produce an economic wave of prosperity that would raise the world's standard of living beyond anything ever dreamed of by man. The hundreds of billions of dollars now spent in mutual preparedness could conceivably abolish poverty from the face of the globe. It could accomplish even more than this; it would at one stroke reduce the international tensions that seem so insurmountable now to matters of more probable solution. For instance, the complex problems of German rearmament, of preventive war, of satellite dominance by major powers, of universal military service, of unconscionable taxation, of nuclear development for industry, of freer exchange of goods and people, of foreign aid and, indeed, of all issues involving the application of armed force. It would have equally potent political effects.

It would reduce immeasurably the power of leaders of government and thus render more precarious totalitarian or autocratic rule. The growing and dangerous control by an individual over the masses—the socialistic and paternal trends resulting therefrom —is largely by virtue of his influence to induce war or to maintain peace. Abolish this threat and the position of Chief Magistrate falls into a more proper civic perspective.

You will say at once that although the abolition of war has been the dream of man for centuries every proposition to that end has been promptly discarded as impossible and fantastic. Every cynic, every pessimist, every adventurer, every swashbuckler in the world has always disclaimed its feasibility. But that was before the science of the past decade made mass destruction a reality. The argument then was along spiritual and moral lines, and lost. It is a sad truth that human character has never reached a theological development which would permit the application of pure idealism. In the last two thousand years its rate of change has been deplorably slow compared to that of the arts and the sciences. But now the tremendous and present evolution of nuclear and other potentials of destruction has suddenly taken the problem away from its primary consideration as a moral and spiritual question and brought it abreast of scientific realism. It is no longer an ethical equation to be pondered solely by learned philosophers and ecclesiastics but a hard core one for the decision of the masses whose survival is the issue. This is as true of the Soviet side of the world as of the free side—as true behind the Iron Curtain as in front of it. The ordinary people of the world, whether free or slave, are all in agreement on this solution; and this perhaps is the only thing in the world they do agree upon. But it is the most vital and determinate of all. The leaders are the laggards. The disease of power seems to confuse and befuddle them. They have not even approached the basic problem, much less evolved a working formula to implement this public demand. They debate and turmoil over a hundred issues—they bring us to the verge of despair or raise our hopes to utopian heights over the corollary misunderstandings that stem from the threat of war—but never in the chancelleries of the world or the halls of the United Nations is the real problem raised. Never do they dare to state the bald truth, that the next great advance in the evolution of civilization cannot take place until war is abolished. It may take another cataclysm of destruction to prove to them this simple truth. But, strange as it may seem, it is known now by all common men. It is the one issue upon which both sides can agree, for it is the one issue upon which both sides will profit equally. It is the one issue—and the only decisive one—in which the interests of both are completely parallel. It is the one issue which, if settled, might settle all others.

Time has shown that agreements between modern nations are generally no longer honored as valid unless both profit therefrom. But both sides can be trusted when both do profit. It becomes then no longer a problem based upon relative integrity. It is now no longer convincing to argue, whether true or not, that we cannot trust the other side—that one maverick can destroy the herd. It would no longer be a matter depending upon trust—the self-interest of each nation outlawing war would keep it true to itself. And there is no influence so potent and powerful as self-interest. It would not necessarily require international inspection of relative armaments—the public opinion of every part of the world would be the great denominator which would ensure the issue—each nation would so profit that it could not fail eventually to comply. This would not, of course, mean the abandonment of all armed forces, but it would reduce them to the simpler problems of internal order and international police. It would not mean Utopia at one fell stroke, but it would mean that the great road block now existing to the development of the human race would have been cleared.

The present tensions with their threat of national annihilation are kept alive by two great illusions. The one, a complete belief on the part of the Soviet world that the capitalist countries are preparing to attack them; that sooner or later we intend to strike. And the other, a complete belief on the part of the capitalistic countries that the Soviets are preparing to attack us; that sooner or later they intend to strike. Both are wrong. Each side, so far as the masses are concerned, is equally desirous of peace. For either side war with the other would mean nothing but disaster.

Both equally dread it. But the constant acceleration of preparation may well, without specific intent, ultimately produce a spontaneous combustion.

I am sure that every pundit in the world, every cynic and hypocrite, every paid brainwasher, every egotist, every trouble-maker, and many others of entirely different mould, will tell you with mockery and ridicule that this can be only a dream—that it is but the vague imaginings of a visionary. But, as David Lloyd George once said in Commons at the crisis of the First World War, "We must go on or we will go under." And the great criticism we can make of the world's leaders is their lack of a plan which will enable us "to go on." All they propose merely gravitates around but dares not face the real problem. They increase preparedness by alliances, by distributing resources throughout the world, by feverish activity in developing new and deadlier weapons, by applying conscription in times of peace— all of which is instantly matched by the prospective opponent. We are told that this increases the chances of peace—which is doubtful—and increases the chances of victory if war comes— which would be incontestable if the other side did not increase in like proportion. Actually, the truth is that the relative strengths of the two change little with the years. Action by one is promptly matched by reaction from the other.

We are told we must go on indefinitely as at present—some say fifty years or more. With what at the end? None say— there is no definite objective. They but pass along to those that follow the search for a final solution. And, at the end, the problem will be exactly the same as that which we face now. Must we live for generations under the killing punishment of accelerating preparedness without an announced final purpose or, as an alternative, suicidal war; and trifle in the meanwhile with corollary and indeterminate theses—such as limitation of armament, restriction on the use of nuclear power, adoption of new legal standards as propounded at Nuremberg—all of which are but palliatives and all of which in varying form have been tried in the past with negligible results? Dangerous doctrines, too, appear—doctrines which might result in actual defeat; such doctrines as a limited war, of enemy sanctuary, of failure to protect our fighting men when captured, of national subversive and sabotage agencies, of a substitute for victory on the battle-field—all in the name of peace. Peace, indeed, can be obtained at least temporarily by any nation if it is prepared to yield its freedom principles. But peace at any price—peace with appease-ment—peace which passes the dreadful finality to future gen-erations—is a peace of sham and shame which can end only in war or slavery.

I recall so vividly this problem when it faced the Japanese in their new Constitution. They are realists; and they are the only ones that know by dread experience the fearful effect of mass annihilation. They realize in their limited geographical area, caught up as a sort of No Man's Land between two great ideol-ogies, that to engage in another war, whether on the winning or the losing side, spells the probable doom of their race. And their wise old Prime Minister, Shidehara, came to me and urged that to save themselves they should abolish war as an international instrument. When I agreed, he turned to me and said, "The world will laugh and mock us as impractical visionaries, but a hundred years from now we will be called prophets."

Sooner or later the world, if it is to survive, must reach this decision. The only question is, when? Must we fight again before we learn? When will some great figure in power have sufficient imagination and moral courage to translate this uni-versal wish—which is rapidly becoming a universal necessity—into actuality? We are in a new era. The old methods and solutions no longer suffice. We must have new thoughts, new ideas, new concepts, just as did our venerated forefathers when they faced a New World. We must break out of the strait-jacket of the past. There must always be one to lead, and we should be that one. We should now proclaim our readiness to abolish war in concert with the great powers of the world. The result would be magical.

This may sound somewhat academic in view of the acuteness of the situation in the Far East. Strategically, the problem there has developed along classical lines—the familiar case of a con-centrated enemy in a central position deployed against scattered allies. Red China, inherently weak in industrial output for modern war but strong in manpower, engaged on three fronts—Korea, Indo-China and in civil war with Nationalist China. Fighting on all three simultaneously meant defeat, but individually the chances were excellent. The hope for victory depended on getting a cease-fire on some fronts so that the full potential of its limited military might could be thrown against the remaining one or ones. That is what has happened and is happening. First was the cessation of the civil war action by the isolation in the Formosa area which practically immobilized Nationalist China, one of the allies. Red China then concentrated against Korea and Indo-China. But even the double front was too much for its strained resources. So a cease-fire was obtained in Korea. This immobilized the so-called United Nations Forces and the South Koreans and left Red China free to concentrate on the third front—Indo-China and the French. Successful there, the Reds now turn back to the old first front located in Formosa. As Napoleon Bonaparte once said: "Give me allies as an enemy so that I can defeat them one by one."

Militarily the situation demonstrates the inherent weakness of the theory of collective security—the chain is no stronger than its weakest link, and what is even more vital—its full power can only be utilized when all links are brought simultaneously into action. The diverse interests of allies always tend towards separation rather than unity.

Whatever betides the ultimate fate of the Far East—and indeed of the world—will not be settled by force of arms. We may all be practically annihilated—but war can no longer be an arbiter of survival.

I cannot close without once more thanking this beautiful city of Los Angeles for its gracious hospitality. It has been an inspiration to be here, where missions once stood as lonely outposts in the advance of our Christian civilization, but where this great metropolis now stands as a monument to American industry and adventure—a symbolic reminder of Californian strength and fortitude. I hate to leave—but, as I once pledged under very different circumstances, I shall return.

UNITED NATIONS AND WORLD OPINION [9]

HENRY CABOT LODGE, JR. [10]

Ambassador Henry Cabot Lodge, Jr., United States Delegate to the United Nations, gave this address to the members of the Associated Press, in New York, on April 19, 1954. The speaker, with much tact and persuasiveness, moved into his theme from broader and less controversial items to his decisive defense of the United Nations and his condemnation of Red China as unfit to join that association of nations. At that time, tension was high concerning the Chinese moves into Indo-China. And a considerable body of opinion in this country and in Europe questioned whether practical politics did not indicate accepting Communist China into the United Nations. Lodge was replying directly to those American isolationists who were continually sniping at this organization.

Ambassador Lodge's speech was broadcast and quickly communicated to the world, including Moscow and Peiping. He thus stated America's official policy concerning the issue of admitting Red China to the United Nations.

Ambassador Lodge, during this period, repeatedly proclaimed this same indictment of Communist China, before the United Nations and elsewhere. He constantly took the propagandistic offensive and, in line with his perception of world opinion, succeeded well in his battles against the unceasing barrages from Russia and her Asian ally.[11]

Public opinion plays such a decisive and fundamental part in every large affair today, and the prospects are that it will play such an increasingly large part in the future, that it is an exceptional privilege for me to have this opportunity to appear before you, the members of the Associated Press, who, by any rational standard, must be ranked among the foremost opinion-makers in our country.

Membership in the Associated Press is a great privilege which is eagerly sought after for the honor and the power which it brings with it. But, as you all know, it brings with it at least

[9] Text furnished through the courtesy of Henry Cabot Lodge, Jr., and the Department of State.

[10] For biographical note, see Appendix.

[11] For comment on Ambassador Lodge as speaker, see *Representative American Speeches: 1950-51*, p37-43; *1952-53*, p25-30.

equivalent responsibilities and these do tend to increase rather than decrease as time goes on.

The position of our country in the field of foreign relations is squarely based on public opinion as are all other activities of our Government. Whenever the conduct of foreign relations gets separated from public opinion, the results are uniformly disastrous. To the extent that the state of public opinion is intelligent and realistic, our foreign policies will be successful; to the extent that public opinion is in error, our foreign policies will be in error. They cannot be disconnected—and that, of course, is where your responsibility as newspaper men directly affects our foreign relations.

Today, let us examine what some basic American attitudes are concerning foreign relations, and then see whether we think these attitudes meet the needs of our present situation.

As a people, we Americans like to solve problems; to overcome obstacles, and to build. It is a national trait. We have been doing these things ever since the foundation of our country and they have become second nature with us. We do not perhaps reflect much on the fact that all problems cannot be solved and that all obstacles cannot be overcome.

We have developed an attitude which to some foreigners seems to be like that of the busy executive who wants to get everything cleaned up in time to catch the 5:15 train. To some of them, Americans are like people who think of the world as a potential tennis court in which all the tapes are stapled down and all the edges neat.

The direct opposite of this attitude exists in certain other parts of the world where many think that the great problems cannot be solved—that they can never be solved—and that the best thing for sensible men to do is to roll with the punch, duck your head when the missiles start flying and generally follow the idea of "eat, drink and be merry for tomorrow we die."

As between these two attitudes, there is no doubt whatever that we are more nearly right and that they are more nearly wrong. Of course, problems can be solved. They are being solved all the time in one way or another. In fact some of them are being solved in such a way that the solution creates a lot of new and more difficult problems. But one thing is certain: the world does not stand still.

Some problems in the past have been brutally solved by war —witness the overthrow of the central European monarchies in World War I, the destruction of fascism, nazism and Japanese imperialism in World War II. To be sure, these events witnessed the rise of communism, which in turn brought immense new problems. These are changes which show that the world does not stand still.

Another great change which all men of my age have seen is the growth of nationalism all over the world. It is one great world fact which in most cases has been accompanied by fighting, some of it on a small scale and some of it to a larger degree.

Many changes have also come about in the world through peaceful means. In fact, the whole face of the world was changed by the discovery of America, which was made in rather primitive sailboats, and has since been followed by steamships, railroads, automobiles and airplanes in the field of transportation, and by telegraphy, radio, motion pictures and television in the field of communications, by medical science, by mass production and by a whole range of other scientific developments.

These peaceful forces of science, commerce and individual effort really do cause far-reaching innovations. Unhappily, it is not often that a far-reaching innovation is brought about in the world exclusively by political and diplomatic means and without fighting. The independence of India is one of those unusual cases. In the last few weeks an event of far-reaching proportions was brought about exclusively by political and diplomatic means. This was the decision of Pakistan to be counted with the free anti-Communist forces of the world and the decision of President Eisenhower to extend military aid to Pakistan. This event and the recently signed agreement with Turkey, of which it is a part, can have a tremendously stabilizing effect in one of the most crucial parts of the world. It is a very real setback for Communist imperialism and should give courage to lovers of freedom in the Near and Middle East—and all over the world. These are examples of statesmanship with a capital S.

But it is not always possible to bring about such basic changes in international relationships by peaceful political and diplomatic means. We Americans make a mistake if we expect too much of the political and diplomatic tools which are available to us. We should not have a sense of failure because there is no peace treaty to conclude World War II in an orderly manner; or because there is no peace treaty establishing permanent relationships in Palestine; or because there is as yet no peace treaty for Korea. We should not be contemptuous of more modest solutions because we overestimate the possibility of curing all the world's ills in one fell swoop.

And we should not get impatient with proceedings of the United Nations or other international gatherings because they talk and do not reach basic solutions of some international questions. To many of these questions there is no basic solution under present conditions. In many of them the choice is: "talk or fight." The fact that the talk may be boring or turgid or uninspiring should not cause us to forget the fact that it is preferable to war.

Now, the wars that don't happen are not dramatic. But there is real satisfaction in working in a place where you feel that sometimes you have helped prevent fighting and bloodshed even if it requires some verbal toe dancing and walking on eggs and what, to most of us, appears to be pettifogging. There are some circumstances in international affairs when the best thing to do is to stall for time and give people a chance to cool off. This often clears the way for diplomacy to exert a moderating and conciliatory influence.

The United Nations has become an accepted instrument of last resort. A state need not feel that it has lost prestige by the reference of its problem to the United Nations. Indeed, a state would lose great prestige if it resisted the United Nations playing its conciliatory role.

This process works even when fighting has already broken out—as in Indonesia, Palestine and Kashmir. The United Nations succeeded in stopping these conflicts—any of which might have engulfed larger areas, or have so disrupted the countries involved as to open the door to communism.

In this respect the United Nations is not—and should not be —a good news source. When one of the world's insoluble problems gets on page one it is practically always because the news is bad. The diplomat who temporizes may be boring and journalistically undesirable, but he is useful in preventing bloodshed.

We Americans are right in our belief that the world changes and that human effort can make it change—and can do it without fighting. The fatalists are wrong when they think mankind is doomed to being blown hither and yon like a cork on the surface of the ocean. But we are wrong if we expect international politics and diplomacy to do much more than fend off the destructive effects of science and invention—and human devilishness.

If a diplomat avoids a crisis he is entitled to the highest commendation. If, by his actions, he avoids a war he has really done all that a diplomat is capable of doing and is entitled to the gratitude of the nation. Let us not expect of diplomacy that which it cannot accomplish. Without giving up our optimism and idealism, which are precious assets to the world, let us learn to live with those things which obviously cannot be altered by peaceful diplomatic methods.

Let us be thankful that we have a place like the United Nations where diplomatic activities can take place which can avoid crises and can prevent war. Let us not hold the United Nations responsible for the fact that it has not been able to remake the world and bring about the millennium by a stroke of the pen. After all, if a powerful government like the United States could not conceivably remake the world, how can we expect an instrument like the United Nations, which has no powers of government, which cannot draft a single soldier, or impose a single tax, to do that which a powerful government cannot do?

Let us appreciate both the capabilities and the limitations of diplomacy. We owe it to ourselves and to our diplomats to appreciate the good work which they do. I have been working with United States career officers in the foreign field for a year and three months and am glad of this opportunity before this influential audience to set down the high opinion which I have of so many of the men and women with whom I have worked and who have spent their lives working for the United States in the field of foreign relations. There has been so much publicity since World War II about a few rotten apples that we have lost sight of the many excellent persons giving service that is not only faithful but skillful in a high degree and utterly indispensable to our survival as a nation.

We all owe a real debt to men like Robert Murphy, who is Deputy Under Secretary of State; David Key, the Assistant Secretary for United Nations Affairs; Livingston Merchant, Assistant Secretary for European Affairs; Henry Byroade, Assistant Secretary for Near Eastern, South Asian and African Affairs; Douglas MacArthur 2d, Counselor for the Department of State. There are forty career Ambassadors—people like George Allen in India, Charles E. Bohlen in the Soviet Union, Jefferson Caffrey in Egypt, James Dunn in Spain, Loy Henderson in Iran, John Cabot in Sweden, James Riddleberger in Yugoslavia, Harold Tittman in Peru and Fletcher Warren in Venezuela—all of these officers and others like them are rendering priceless service to their country in posts which call for the exercise of the most exquisite judgment and which require a knowledge of how to get things done in foreign countries which is possessed by very few Americans.

If we did not have officials like them we would be in very serious trouble. I wish we had more of them, and I hope that young men and women of similar quality from one end of our nation to the other will plan to make a career in the field of foreign relations so that for the future of our country we will have a supply of these indispensable public officials.

The United Nations is one great factor in the field of foreign relations which must have particular meaning for a newspaper man—and I speak as one who still considers himself to be basically a member of that profession. The powers of the United Nations to take actions which are legally binding are very few in number. They are limited exclusively to the Security Council, where the United States is completely protected by the right of veto. The overwhelming majority of United Nations actions are purely recommendatory. The reason that they have such great weight is because of the force of public opinion—in this case world opinion.

And world public opinion, while it does not react as rapidly as public opinion does in an American city or state or in the United States, is, nevertheless, a very real force.

It was world opinion which was so informed and stimulated by the proceedings in the United Nations in 1946 that the Soviet Union withdrew the troops which they had in northern Iran which were a very real threat to the integrity of that country and to the entire region, a region which is so highly strategic to the interests of our country, as well as to the interests of the people who live there.

It was the force of world opinion, which was again stimulated by the United Nations, which made our resistance to Communist aggression in Korea considerably more than it would have been if the United Nations had never existed.

The contribution of the United Nations to our resistance to Communist aggression in Korea is not limited to the fact that it added two divisions which we would have otherwise had to supply ourselves and which would have cost us $600 million a year—and this figure, when compared to our contribution of $13 million a year to the United Nations proper, does not seem like a bad deal.

The contribution of the United Nations to our resistance to aggression in Korea is not limited to the fact that the presence of those two divisions meant that other young men risked becoming casualties which otherwise might have been the fate of American boys.

Those are worth-while contributions—and they could have been even larger if mistaken policies had not been followed in Washington in those years—policies which required countries having military manpower, but not having dollars, to reimburse us in dollars for the supplies and equipment which we provided. This deprived us of the manpower which otherwise would have been available. It was a reversal of World War II policy. It is a mistake, by the way, which will not be repeated in the future.

But these things, although of the first importance, are not all that the United Nations contributed to resisting aggression in Korea.

The fact that the United Nations condemned Communist aggression at once made the whole action one based on principle and not on American strategic self-preservation. This completely foiled the Communist propaganda line that action in Korea was controlled by the power politics of the Wall Street imperialists.

Another valuable result of United Nations intervention which would also never have taken place without the United Nations was due to the fact that soldiers of so many races, religions and colors, including such widely separated nations as Turkey, Ethiopia, Thailand, the Philippines and Colombia, among the total sixteen, were in the battle line. It thus became impossible for the Communists to maintain successfully that our action in Korea was another example of the white man trying to dominate colored people and reestablish colonialism.

Iran and Korea are two illustrations of what public opinion can do when it is rallied as it was at the United Nations.

The United Nations serves many other useful purposes in the field of public opinion.

It is, for one thing, a place where you can get the feel of world opinion. On one occasion Mr. [Andrei Y.] Vishinsky, with upraised fist, turned to me and said, "You Americans have lost Asia." I made the obvious retort that we Americans weren't trying to get Asia, that we did not regard Asia as a mere pawn in the game of power politics; that we regarded Asians as human beings—to be treated with the respect to which human beings are entitled. After I made this statement representatives of countries in the Far East told me that it would make a hit with their editors and political leaders and that it should be translated into the appropriate languages and sent out over the Voice of America. That is the type of reaction which cannot be obtained in any other way and which you as newspaper men will appreciate.

The United Nations is a forum which can be used to refute lies. Many of you remember, I am sure, the dramatic presentation which was made by Dr. Charles Mayo last fall, showing in detail the falsity of Communist charges that United States soldiers had used germ warfare in Korea. Dr. Mayo's presentation made the front page both at home and abroad over a ten-day period.

The United Nations is a forum in which to develop the truth, however dreadful it may be, about the Soviet Union. We aired the reports in the United Nations about the Soviet treatment of Germans, Japanese and Italian World War II prisoners. When an impartial commission, headed by a distinguished Indian, made scientific and objective findings about forced labor behind the Iron Curtain, we used the world forum of the United Nations as the place in which to bring them before world opinion.

The United Nations is a place to develop the truth, however awful it may be, about the Chinese Communists. We have consistently stressed that the Chinese Communist regime is unfit for representation in the United Nations:

Because it has repeatedly expressed open contempt for the purpose and principles of the United Nations, and for judgments of the international community.

Because it stands convicted by the United Nations as an aggressor in Korea, where it killed and wounded many thousands of American and other soldiers who were defending peace.

Because it continues to support aggression in Indo-China, by giving substantial aid and by furnishing advisers and technicians to the Viet-Minh forces.

Because it occupied defenseless Tibet and seized control of its Government and resources.

Because it sponsors guerrilla and subversive movements in Malaya and throughout the rest of Southeast Asia.

Because it committed dreadful atrocities against Americans and others fighting for the United Nations in Korea and subjected prisoners to physical and mental cruelty in seeking to extort military secrets and confessions of alleged guilt.

Because it still holds thirty-two American civilians under barbarous conditions with published charges and subjects these innocent missionaries, journalists and businessmen to cruel and inhuman treatment.

Because it willfully fabricated and publicized false evidence of spurious germ warfare charges designed to blacken the reputation of the United States, and otherwise carries on a deliberate "hate America" propaganda campaign.

Because it has executed millions of its captive subjects, and forced other millions into slave labor.

Because it even stoops to an international extortion racket in squeezing millions of dollars from overseas Chinese who try to buy safety and protection for their relatives at home.

The exposure of the terrible ways in which the Chinese Communists violate the normally accepted standards of international conduct has so horrified many decent people that this regime has never even gotten a toehold on the threshold of the United Nations. Since 1949, United Nations bodies have refused over 150 times to seat the Chinese Communists. I can promise you that the United States will steadfastly resist all maneuvers by the Chinese Communist regime and its advocates to bribe its way into the United Nations on more promises of good behavior in the future. To admit to the United Nations this regime, which believes in war as an instrument of national policy, would be the first time in its history that the United Nations had deliberately decided to stultify itself by flagrantly acting in contradiction of its primary and basic purpose to "save succeeding generations from the scourge of war."

The United Nations is a place in which the world initiative can be seized. We lost that initiative—or rather we threw it away—at the end of hostilities of World War II. On December 8 last year, President Eisenhower, speaking in the United Nations, made his plea for an international stockpile of fissionable material to be used for peaceful purposes. As James Reston, the diplomatic expert of the New York *Times*, said, "The President put the Kremlin more on the defensive than at any time since the war."

Most of us can remember a few short years back when the Soviets held the indisputable initiative in the cold war. Do you remember the so-called "Stockholm Peace Appeal"—a fake petition device of a kind which is familiar to every small-town editor in this country but which deluded quite a few of the gullible in other countries? Do you remember Picasso's Communist peace pigeon?

Now it is we who have taken the initiative and it is our President who has made his statesmanlike offer. It is accordingly they who stand before the world as the warlike ones.

In conclusion, I have given you these few illustrations, believing that as newspaper men we can appreciate the value of having a world forum. The United Nations is the only real world forum. If you have an idea which you want to get spread around the world, the quickest way to get it spread is through the United Nations. Next to the tall building you will see a low, rather sway-backed building which to me resembles a loudspeaker. That is the General Assembly of the United Nations, and if the architect intended it to resemble a loudspeaker he had the right idea. And I would remind you that if we have not got the gumption and the intelligence and the imagination to use this loudspeaker, it is our fault and not the fault of the loudspeaker.

All these outbreaks in Iran, in Israel, in India, in Pakistan, in Korea and elsewhere—would probably have mushroomed into World War III if the United Nations had not existed, and, if this had happened, no one can estimate what the cost would have been in money and blood. The United Nations, primitive and evolutionary thought it is, has a notable record of accomplishment—both as an actual war preventive and as a forum in the cold war. Let us work together to make it better.

ECONOMIC POLICIES

OUR FOREIGN ECONOMIC POLICY[1]

CLARENCE B. RANDALL [2]

Clarence B. Randall, chairman of the Inland Steel Company, gave this address before the thirty-sixth annual meeting of the American Farm Bureau Federation, at the Hotel New Yorker, New York, on December 14, 1954.

The speaker, talking extemporaneously and with few notes, produced his usual "sharp effect." As president of the Inland Steel Company since 1949, as Paul Hoffman's adviser in the Economic Cooperation Administration, and as chairman of President Eisenhower's Commission on Foreign Economic Policy that recommended a reduction of tariffs in the years 1952-1954, and later, Mr. Randall spoke out of much experience as industrialist and economic investigator. He had also unusual skill in public speaking and adjustment to his many audiences.

This address, for example, illustrates his method of relating his ideas and appeals to the auditors before him. Present is a strong personal quality (numerous "I's" and "you's"); humor and pleasantry ("I have just left my plow in the furrow"); orderly structure (successive development of the attention, need, satisfaction, and action steps of his discourse); informality of oral language ("He yells; his trade association yells; his congressman yells"); direct dialogue; numerous questions; and constant insertion of concrete examples.

These persuasive elements are controlled and enhanced by a rapid and dominating delivery. Mr. Randall has established himself as an outstanding speaker in the interests of the moderately liberal wing of business and industry.[3]

Mr. Chairman, Mr. Ambassador [Sir Roger Makins, of Great Britain], and Ladies and Gentlemen: I hope nobody expects a finished address from me this afternoon such as you will have heard from Sir Roger. I just left my plow in the furrow and came over here.

[1] A stenographic transcript of the address of December 4, 1954. Text through the courtesy of Mr. Clarence Randall, with permission for this reprint.

[2] For biographical note, see Appendix.

[3] See also *Representative American Speeches: 1951-52*, p 112-23.

It has been a very mad sort of day for me because, as you may know, this is the day when the President is meeting with the leaders of both parties to discuss the bipartisan aspects of the legislative program in the coming year. I had to be in Washington this morning to present to that group the subject which I shall endeavor to present to you.

I have seen some bad days in Washington but it was very, very bad today. My plane was an hour late in getting away. And when we got here, lo and behold, the plane was lost over LaGuardia, and we spent about three-quarters of an hour over Flatbush, in the soup.

So here I am without lunch, but many a farmer has gone without lunch. I am happy to be with you.

There are a great many reasons why I am happy to be here today. It is a great privilege for me to share the platform with a man for whom I have such deep respect as I have for the British Ambassador. It has been my privilege to know him for years. His knowledge of world affairs and the depth of his experience mean a great deal at this time in holding our two countries into common focus.

I don't know whether you know, Sir Roger, but I am essentially a Yorkshireman.

[Sir Roger interrupted: "So am I."]

Two Yorkshiremen! It does so happen that my Yorkshire blood has been distilled through seven generations of American farmers on both sides. I happen to be the first male member of my family on either side in as long as there have been ancestors who was not a farmer. And I am carrying out the well-known principle of agriculture. I am letting it lie fallow for one generation.

I don't think anything is wrong, is there, if an American farmer's family gives one man out of every seven generations to the steel industry?

And then I am here today to express my own sense of personal obligation to your great organization for the things I believe so deeply these days. I am sure you all remember how, in your program for 1953, you proposed the establishment of what became the Commission on Foreign Economic Policy, of which I had the great privilege of being chairman by appointment from the President. I have always believed that one of the strong forces that brought that project into being was the great imagination and creative leadership of Allan Kline, who believed in it so deeply.

The news that you have had today about this great American moved me deeply. [Mr. Kline had just announced his retirement for reasons of health.] I left the President but a few hours ago and I am sure he did not know, and I am sure he will be distressed to know, that at this critical time this man's leadership must be withdrawn; but he will join, I am sure, with you and with me in wishing the best forever to this great citizen, Allan Kline.

I am going to talk to you about the President's foreign economic policy and his program in the coming year. I ought to express the caution at the outset that this is Randall and not Eisenhower speaking. This is my interpretation. The President is quite able to give his own interpretation in his own way at his own time. This is just straight Randall this afternoon.

I have always been impressed with that phrase the President coined, in which he said, "The United States bears an awesome responsibility in the world today." This is not of our own seeking, but whatever we do and whatever we say, or whatever we fail to do and fail to say, does have a profound effect on the free world. There is no turning back of that clock and we must face up to our responsibilities.

In the economic field, it is perfectly clear that the world is out of joint. There is serious distortion today. For example, the entire world is our market. The entire world wants to buy our manufactured goods and wants particularly to buy our agricultural produce; but the world can't pay for it. Some way must be found whereby the rest of the world may earn its way in its relationship with us.

After the war, Western Europe was in a state that had to be seen to be believed. For the third time in my life—and in the life of you others who, like myself, stand in the shadow of senility—for the third time, I say, the world had been torn apart by great conflict. And Western Europe had seen its manufacturing equipment plants destroyed, the best of its men taken, its liquid capital consumed to keep the fight going. There they were at the end of last war; and the Marshall Plan came into being.

I have never felt that the Marshall Plan was in any sense a partisan question. I believe that whichever party had been in power and whoever had been in the White House, there would have been a Marshall Plan. As I said the other evening, when I was speaking to the National Association of Manufacturers, there were faults of administration; we ought to know because most of us were there and committed the errors. But whatever may have been the faults of administration, I for one believe that the Marshall Plan saved the free world. It snatched back France, Italy, and other countries from the fate that befell Czechoslovakia and Poland and the other Soviet nations, and it stopped that hard march of Communism.

But that was an abnormal thing for the economies of the world. We were pouring out values from this country to the full tune of $40 billion over the years, for which we had no corresponding flow from the other direction, obviously. It gave us a false sense of prosperity. In that respect, it gave you farmers a false sense of prosperity, because during that period of time we were lifting ourselves by our bootstraps. Your produce went overseas and it was paid for by the American taxpayer who had given the funds to other nations with which to buy; and that gave you high incomes. It was reflected in the farm implement industry. I ought to know because we were selling them a lot of steel at the time and our plate mills and flat roll mills and bar roll mills ran at capacity, supplying materials which you were buying. All the time, the American taxpayer was paying the bills, and we didn't have quite the sense to think it through and see that obvious fact.

Now, that had to stop. It has stopped. The period of large economic grants-in-aid is over and the question facing the world today is whether something can be found by which the world may earn its way in its relationship with the United States.

I say to you that unless the present great imbalance in world trade, the shortage of dollars, can be corrected, you, the farmer, will feel it more than any other group.

You must export to live, and you cannot export unless there is the wherewithal to buy, for, obviously, trade must be two-way. And many of my friends in industry seem to be under the hallucination that we can go on forever exporting, and, at the same time, forbid imports.

The laws of trade and of economics are inexorable and what goes out must be matched by what comes in. That's what the President's program is about. It will be offered to the new Congress in substantially the same form as you will find written in his message to Congress last year, dated March 30. And that program is a package that isn't just a tariff; it is many, many things besides that. It is a program which attempts to throw the economic power of the United States into restoring sanity to the world economy; trying, if you will, to release in the world the forces which have made America great. Those forces are brought into effect by: reliance upon private initiative, vigorous competition, and free markets.

Now, the first step in that program is to try to bring about a strong flow of American capital abroad into the underdeveloped parts of the world—capital that goes out into the world for gain. It is to be hoped that Americans will invest in other parts of the world because they will make money by so doing. Well, there are many road blocks to that. Some of those road blocks exist in other countries and the United States must use its influence to try to bring to pass a more favorable climate or environment for the investment of our funds than exists.

A little over a year ago, my wife and I had the great adventure of going to Turkey on behalf of the Government. My mission was to ascertain what, in a country like Turkey, causes Americans to hesitate to invest. I cannot burden you with all of the reasons, but there were many strange circumstances.

The government of Turkey, for example, has no laws comparable to ours for the organization of a corporation by which the savings of a great many people may be brought together to provide financial backing for a venture. Your Turk, like so many people in the underdeveloped parts of the world, never tells anybody what his assets are; he doesn't even tell his wife. (Well, there are Americans that have that problem, but—.)

In this country, when we organize a corporation, we turn to a certified public accountant who examines our books and says, "These are the assets." I found that in Turkey there isn't one certified public accountant.

But there are also road blocks to foreign investment in our own country. The President, for example, is advocating that in order to give an incentive for the outward flow of capital, that corporations who invest abroad be given a credit of 14 percentage points on their corporate income tax for income earned in foreign countries.

Well, so much for investment. Another very important medium for helping to restore balance to world trade is tourism. People once took that subject a little lightly, but travel has become the American's obsession.

My wife and I were in Europe a few weeks ago and almost everywhere we went we met people that we knew. We'd say, "What in the world are you doing in Europe?"

"Oh, we're here because Joe is stationed in Germany and he has two weeks off and we're going to take a trip with him."

As a matter of fact, the GI went everywhere in the world. He came back and now Papa and Mama and Nellie, they all want to go to the places the GI went. And the Americans have the airplanes and the ships to take them, and all of those dollars serve eventually to come back to us to provide a market for American goods.

In the last analysis, however, you have to face squarely up to the question of tariffs.

On tariffs, the story goes like this: Whoever imposes a high tariff to restrict the import of goods thereby restricts the export of goods. When you hear of some manufacturer asking for a higher tariff on his product, please remember he is asking that less wheat, less cotton, less tobacco, less rice to be shipped out of the United States.

And there is the economics of tariffs in a nutshell, my friends. High protection to restrict imports is, in fact, the restriction of exports. The difference is that competition for domestic manufacturers comes home to him quickly; he knows when it hits. He yells; his trade association yells; his congressman yells; and great to-do takes place. But if there is alongside his factory another that ships its product overseas no one puts a sign on that plant when it cuts back employment to four days a week because the countries to which it sells are not allowed to earn the dollars with which to buy, nobody hears about it. You don't identify the cause and effect.

Now, after the war, the American manufacturer said to the Government, "Take off controls. What we need is to get government out of business. Let the free forces of private initiative and the free market govern and we will put on a show." And the Government did take off controls.

Yet, when industry asks for higher tariffs, it is asking the Government to come back into business. It is asking for government controls, because then a bureaucrat decides who in the economy shall have a benefit and who a disadvantage. Man-made judgments are substituted for the law of economics. And I say to you that nobody imposes a high tariff to benefit one manufacturer who doesn't thereby damage another section of the economy.

Since you and I are farmers today—me by inheritance and you actually—I will give you some examples right out of your subject. I hope they don't hurt, but I am not accustomed to pulling my punches.

Let me give you an example, which I think is quite a classic on how not to behave in a country. After the war we needed Denmark in the free world, and Denmark was close to the starvation point. We sent a mission to Denmark, and that mission said, "We want your help very much. We particularly want some air bases in the Baltic. What can we do?"

Denmark said, "We would like to ship some blue cheese to the United States."

We said, "You are silly. You don't know how to package blue cheese. You'll never enter our markets. You have never met the American housewife." So a million dollars of Marshall Plan money was spent to teach the Danes how to enter the American market with cheese.

And they said, "O.K., what do you want?"

We said, "We want two things. We want an air base in the Baltic and we want you to buy American coal."

They said, "O.K." So the million dollars was spent.

Thereafter, the American Congress, in its infinite wisdom, excluded blue cheese. So what happened? We lost the million dollars. We lost the air bases forever in the Baltic and the Danes bought Polish coal. The net result of that was to bring prosperity to Wisconsin and distress to West Virginia.

Another one happened two weeks ago to which perhaps you can tell me the answer. We have excluded the Dutch dairy products to protect the American farmer. I talked about industry last week; I am talking about farmers today. We excluded Dutch dairy products.

Two weeks ago in Geneva, in the negotiations going on there over GATT (General Agreement on Tariffs and Trade), the Dutch said, "No dairy products, huh? Then there will be no wheat flour made of American wheat coming into Holland," and they have excluded it. So the wheat farmer is picking up the check for the dairy farmer.

Take the importation of oats. That was a terribly hot subject with you and with me and with everybody. I practically grew up in an oat field in New York State. I know all about oats. Canada was quite nettled about our position resisting the importation of oats. And Canada is a great market for citrus fruit. Canada now says, "No oats, no citrus fruit."

In the administration of the tariffs, somebody in government, my friends, has to make the decisions as to whether Government is going to favor the oat farmer or the citrus grower.

I could stand here all afternoon citing examples. Take the coal industry. The coal industry wants to exclude residual fuel oil from Venezuela, because it says it is destroying its market for coal. Yet, the same coal industry, in the same convention, passed a resolution asking that fuel oil from Venezuela be restricted, and a second one demanding that the State Department compel Belgium, France, and Germany to reduce their tariffs and open the markets to American coal. You can't ride both those horses. I mean, you may be a trick rider, but you can't ride both of those horses at the same time.

Supposing we did exclude residual fuel oil from Venezuela. What would happen? There's another principle about the tariffs. The American citizen does not realize the extent to which other countries possess power to hurt the United States and that they will use it.

Now, Venezuela happens to have the most rapidly rising standard of living in the world today. It is a fabulous market for American consumer durables such as refrigerators and electric stoves and what have we. All right! They buy them with the dollars they get for the oil; so we cut off the oil. We therefore cut off the dollars with which our products are being bought.

Well, Venezuela won't take that lying down. It wants its people to have those things and it has a perfectly easy way to get the dollars. All it has to do is levy an export tax on the iron ore that flows from its mines to Bethlehem Steel Company and United States Steel Corporation on the East Coast, and it will have the same dollars and the American people will pay the bill just the same through the increased price of steel.

Take the Swiss watch decision. I expect probably to be stopped at the border next time I try to visit Switzerland and excluded as an undesirable alien, because I was on the President's staff at the time he made the decision to give protection to Swiss watches. I won't go into that today; the reasons were sound in my judgment.

Nevertheless, you are the people that take the shock for the protection to the Swiss watches. How do you like it? Switzerland last year bought four times as much from the United States as we bought from Switzerland, and what is it going to cut down on? It is going to cut down on tobacco from the South and lard from Kansas. That's the present position of the Swiss. Are you people ready to give up your markets in order to maintain the watch industry in the States in the volume to which it believes it is entitled?

Every such decision of that kind, my friends, is an interference with the natural laws of the free market and constitutes, therefore, the same kind of intrusion of government into business and the same establishment of controls that we have resisted.

Now, I submit that the President's program in the tariff field is reasonable and moderate and one calculated not to damage the American economy. He will ask from the next Congress the right, over a three-year period, to reduce tariffs on selected commodities by 5 per cent per year. And it would be a strange business, indeed in the United States, that couldn't survive that 5 per cent change in the competitive prive. And I submit that that is moderate, evolutionary, gradual program, and headed in the right direction.

Don't forget, whereas every special group in the United States that has an interest to protect is vocal and has a high-paid staff in Washington to protect its interests, the great groups in America that are unprotected are the consumer groups, and I am facing such a group. There is no organized group in the United States to protect the buyer, but great organization to protect the seller.

I will make one exception. There is one organized group to protect the buyer and that's organized women; and may God bless the women forever for standing up as they have been, to be heard on the subject.

I am frequently told that we need a high tariff to protect the standard of living in America, and I have never been able to see how it would protect your standard of living to make you pay more for your merchandise. The American farmer's wife is accustomed to buying where she can buy best and cheapest, and it makes no sense to me that a group of bureaucrats, if you will, whom she has never seen, shall have the power to tell her what she must buy and what not to buy, and to tell her to pay a higher price to protect some people she has never seen, and be happy to do it.

Well, so much for the tariff. I could go on indefinitely, but if your goods are to be bought abroad, more European goods—more world goods—must come into the United States, and that is that.

This problem, of course, has certain very special phases. We are facing in the next few weeks and months the very serious problem of what to do about Japan. The plight of Japan is desperate. True, she was our enemy; but today she is essential to the security of our nation. Should Japan go the other way, we couldn't take it. Add her potential in ship-building, in munitions, steel and heavy industry to that of the Soviet world and there would be an immediate threat, not only to the Philippines, but to Hawaii, Alaska and eventually directly to our own shores. We cannot take that risk. And Japan at the present time is $600 million a year short of making her living; and we have terminated aid.

She hasn't enough agricultural capacity to feed her population. She must import food. She hasn't enough raw materials for her factories; she must import those; and she lives by the skill of her people.

The free world must join together to find a way to absorb enough Japanese goods to their markets to permit Japan to have a way of life or she will go the other way and will cultivate her historic and traditional markets, which are those of the Soviet bloc.

And on the same line of reasoning, we have the controversial question of East-West trade. For any discussion of this subject it must first be delimited. No one for a moment advocates trade with the East that involves materiel of war, and no one advocates trade with China. Our defense people feel that at the moment that is improper, and I for one accept their judgment.

In between lies a great area of possible strength for our allies, and this is the way I see it:

Traditionally—all through the centuries, Western Europe traded with the East. It was in the West that industry developed. It shipped eastward manufactured products and received in return the grains and the products of the forest and raw materials. After the war we said, "Uh-uh! no can do." And they said, "Well, how can that be? How can we live, if you take our markets away?"

We said, "Relax, we'll send you a check." So every year we sent them a check and that was swell. Finally we send them a check and say, "By the way, it may interest you to know, this is the last check."

Well, they said, "What do we do now? How do we live?"

And we said, "Well, we're sorry. That will be your prob-lem. We've got to catch a plane. We are needed back home," and we dumped them. We cut off their traditional markets and we won't let them enter our markets, and we ask them thereby to reduce their standard of living, all for the priceless privilege of standing at our side in the battle of democracy, and it makes no sense to me.

I say we ought to encourage our allies in Western Europe to resume their traditional markets in the East and outsmart the opposition. And I believe that peace follows trade, that the more times we penetrate the curtain by people who are there to pursue their own interest, the more fresh air we let in, the better chance there is of ultimate adjustment.

Well, I could go on outlining these various issues for you. Sir Roger spoke of the great problem of convertibility in the world. Convertibility means arriving at such a state in the world where a man may readily convert pounds into dollars or marks into lira, and have complete freedom of choice as to where he will invest his money, what he will do with his money. That is not possible today. That is not because the British Common-wealth is unwilling to do the right and reasonable thing, but because the attitude of the United States on this trade question compels it to take steps which it does not like to take.

Reflect on this a moment. This morning a rather important gentleman—a member of the Congress—said to me, "But don't forget all the tariff barriers and quotas and other regimentation that other nations are placing upon us."

I don't forget it for a minute; it keeps me awake nights. But the reason they are opposing these things is because dollars are short.

Where a nation cannot get all the dollars that its people wish to employ, that nation has to ration dollars. First it has to make them last through the year; and it has to see that those dollars are used for the essentials and not for the luxuries. That is why nations impose quotas and why they regiment our trade with them.

I have businessmen say to me, "There's only one problem; that's convertibility. Why don't they settle convertibility?"

You can't settle convertibility unless you settle trade; unless, basically, the trade relationships between countries are in balance. No gold reserve would stand against the drain.

Conversely, if the things we sell and the things all the world sells to us are approximately in balance, anybody can arrive at convertibility.

I have great respect for the position taken by the Chancellor of the Exchequer of Great Britain [Richard A. Butler] when he was in Washington last September. I can understand perfectly when he says that the whole world waits for the United States to make up its mind whether it is going to enter freely into partnership with the world in the economic sphere, or whether the world must wall itself off against the United States.

But don't let anybody tell you that convertibility is a separate question from the adjustment of trade. It's the hen and the egg, and this time I know which comes first. There must be balance in trade between nations before those nations can have their currency freely converted.

Now, in all this, there is no problem that looms larger than that of agriculture. We cannot have a sound foreign economic policy unless we have a sound policy in agriculture, and I can't tell you what admiration I have for your leadership and for this great group for facing up squarely up to that question.

Here's one thing that confronts me when I talk to manufacturers. When I meet with men in industry, the first thing they say is, "What are you doing about 'dumping'? When are you going to tighten up the dumping laws?"

You all know what dumping means. If a foreign country, in order to get its goods introduced here over our tariff, rebates a part of the cost to the exporter, whether directly or indirectly, that is dumping. It is unfair competition for the Government to assume part of that cost of export, and every American manufacturer yells, and properly yells, when dumping takes place.

And yet, when people suggest, my friends, that agricultural products be sold in the world market at less than the price that our Government pays, that is dumping; and we can't have it both ways. We have to find in all of these subjects principles that apply to all people in the nation alike, and if it's dumping when the manufacturers do it, it's dumping when it's the produce of agriculture. We've got to find some sound principles to which we can adhere; and of course I need not say that these great problems in our country will never be settled until every citizen, whether he is a manufacturer, a farmer, or a laborer in a plant, is willing to look first at the national interest and secondly at his own interest.

The very survival of the democratic way of life, in my judgment, hinges upon our rising to that height where we can make every decision in life in terms of what is best for the country before we consider our own self-interest. Or to put it the other way—I like to put it this way—we must be intelligent enough to know that what is best for the country is, in the last analysis, the only thing that is good for us.

It is a great subject, my friends. It is complex; it is difficult to comprehend; and it is sometimes so remote that it does not touch our daily lives. And yet I ask you to believe that when the President puts the subject of foreign economic policy at the top of his list of priorities, as he will, that he knows what he's doing. And I ask you to study, I ask you to inform yourselves about it. I ask you to review it with a fresh start and with open minds because the whole future of our country is involved in two respects:

One is our military security. We have been maintaining the economic strength of our allies. We have now stopped doing that. So they must have a new strength that they themselves have earned. Our allies must be economically strong.

The second is that America may go on having an ever-rising standard of living and an increased volume of production. For that she must have the world for her market.

I am about through. I am about to go to lunch, but I want to say this too. I know you people. I grew up in a small town. I know and love that integrity that is found among farming people everywhere. And I always used to think that farmers, when they got excited, did something. Try to put something over on a farmer and he will follow you for ten miles.

I wish you would approach this subject in that spirit. If you believe in what I have presented to you this afternoon; if you believe as I do with the greatest depth of conviction I can command, that the welfare of the American farmer hinges upon getting world trade in balance, go out and fight for it.

No great reform ever came about automatically. Truth needs help. The voice of self-interest in our country today is very articulate. The voice of the good citizen on this subject is not yet roused.

If you believe in this program, do something about it, and the first thing to do is to tell your congressman.

PARTY POLITICS

REPUBLICAN PRECINCT DAY RALLY [1]

DWIGHT D. EISENHOWER [2]

President Dwight D. Eisenhower, casting aside for the hour his nonpartisan character, delivered this address before a G.O.P. rally at the City Auditorium, Denver, Colorado, on October 8, 1954. The speech was televised and broadcast to some 692 stations throughout the nation. The President was seen and heard by some 2,150,000 party workers and friends in some 26,500 party caucuses and rallies across the country (these figures supplied by the Republican National Committee).

The address in this case was the outcome of a week of conferences between President Eisenhower and his party leaders—who reported that the campaign was moving slowly and that the President's voice and appeal were necessary to stimulate the party and all voters. The Gallup poll reported that outside the South, the Republican candidates for Congress held only a 51 per cent lead, whereas a 55 per cent G.O.P. vote was necessary to assure control of Congress. During the day of the broadcast, the President conferred at length with Vice President Nixon, Joe Martin, Charles Halleck, Leonard Hall, and other directors of party strategy. "Ike" also completed his political speech.

As the campaign entered the closing days of October the President became more and more active on the political stump and over national radio and television channels. Never before had a President campaigned so vigorously in a mid-term election. He worked hard, as did all other Republican campaigners to emphasize the major issue, "a vote for your Republican governor or congressman is a vote for Eisenhower." During a single day at the end of October, he "airhopped" with speeches at Cleveland, Ohio; Louisville, Kentucky; and Wilmington, Delaware.

The election results, with both House and Senate Democratic, were variously interpreted. Was Eisenhower's speaking campaign a failure? If he had remained aloof, the Democratic tide would have been much higher. His vigorous appeals were generally credited with averting a larger Democratic majority.

The President continues to speak with directness. He makes no pretense at oratory, and often develops a monotony of vocal pattern as he reads. But his voice and visible manner continue to convey sincerity and have been important in helping him to retain strong popularity.[3]

[1] Text furnished through the courtesy of the Republican National Committee.

[2] For biographical note, see Appendix.

[3] For further comment on President Eisenhower as a speaker, see the Index of this volume for his addresses since 1944.

Governor Thornton, Mr. Vice President, distinguished leaders of the Congress, members of this great audience, and my good friends, over all of America:

Tonight, as I speak to my countrymen, I am privileged to address myself especially to my fellow Republican workers, gathered here in Denver and in meetings throughout our land. To each of you—to your families, to your friends, and to your political associates—I send my warmest greetings.

All of us are happy that tonight Mr. Nixon, Speaker Joe Martin, and the other members of our able legislative team are here with us. Under the leadership of these men, the Eighty-third Congress made its record of extraordinary success. They have my respect and admiration for the splendid service they have rendered to the American people.

Tonight, in our meetings over America, we come together as members of the Republican party. But in spirit we have also with us the vast army of other Americans who in 1952, and since, have fought alongside us for the great plans and programs for which together we stand.

We assemble here, and all over America, proud of our party's principles—proud of our party's record.

Now, what are these principles and that record, and as Republicans, what is our goal?

That goal is not political power for its own sake, but to advance the good of 163 million Americans.

To that end, we are dedicated to the maximum of individual freedom, fostered by a government desiring not to dominate but only to serve—a government kept close to the hearthsides of America—a government liberal in dealing with the human concerns of the people, but conservative in spending their money. From Lincoln's day to this these have been the fundamental aims of our historic party.

Republicans believe that such government will best preserve liberty and justice, and prosperity and happiness in our land.

Such a government will best promote an enduring peace throughout the world.

These are the convictions that unite us; this is the cause that inspires us—and our friends—to continued and dedicated effort.

Two years ago the people of our country showed their desire for this kind of government.

Remember Election Day 1952. In the early hours of morning, in thousands of precincts over America, our citizens eagerly lined up to vote long before the polls were open.

Do you remember why Americans crowded to the polls on November 4, 1952?

Let's think back.

Two years ago Americans wanted an end to the war in Korea. It was a costly war, allowed to become futile, and seemingly without end.

They wanted something done about our veterans, who suddenly found the country so poorly prepared that they themselves had once again to undergo the dangers of battle, while others remained at home who had never served.

Americans wanted a government thrifty and frugal with the public's money.

They wanted a stop to the endless rise in taxes, taking more and more of the family income to support an overgrown Washington bureaucracy.

They wanted something done about inflation—to end the growing discouragement as day by day pensions and savings and the weekly pay check bought less and less at the corner store.

Americans were determined to eliminate penetration by the Communist conspiracy in our government and in our whole society. They did not consider this menace a red herring.

They wanted clean, honest government.

They were anxious to get rid of the antagonism between the Congress and the Executive which hamstrung the processes of government.

All this America wanted two years ago, and you—you, and those like you throughout this great nation—did something about it.

You remember the telephone brigades of two years ago. You remember the "Get Out the Vote" campaigns. You remember the drive, the enthusiasm that in November 1952, surged forth from our people.

And what happened? You got results.

The people of America established in Washington the kind of government they wanted.

In just twenty months, we have come far.

First of all, with the help of thousands of citizens from every walk of life and from every part of America, we devised a comprehensive, progressive program in keeping with the Republican party's platform and the pledges made to America during the campaign. Fundamentally, that program has but one purpose—to make America stronger and better, with growing prosperity and happiness for all of our people.

Now, that program was made up of many parts affecting every phase of the life of our great nation. Some parts could be accomplished quickly. Others necessarily had to be developed slowly over the months, to assure their fitness and effectiveness. Important sections still remain to be enacted. The program is one, therefore, of continuous and simultaneous study and action. Its completion is essential to the future prosperity, security and peace of the people of America.

So, let's consider this program and what has happened since its inception.

Fourteen months ago, the futile sacrifices in Korea were stopped.

We now have clean, honest, decent government in Washington.

Government spending has been sharply reduced. Stifling controls have been removed from our nation's economy, amid dire predictions of carping critics that inflation would follow and prices would soar out of sight.

In twenty months, this Administration and the Republican-led Congress cut our government's costs by $11 billion.

And at last, we have a tax cut!

Taxes were cut $7.4 billion—the largest tax cut in the history of this nation. It brings benefits to every family in every American home.

At the same time, we smoked out 211 thousand unnecessary positions on the Federal payrolls.

All during this time, our government has been returning to private citizens activities traditionally belonging to private citizens.

It is stopping the roasting of coffee, the baking of bread, the making of paint and clothes. It has stopped running a hotel. It has stopped running a tug and barge business on our inland waterways. In keeping with the philosophy of our whole program, all of these activities have been returned to private citizens —exactly where they belong.

My friends, I could never mention this subject without adverting to a statement of our first and greatest leader, Lincoln. He said, "The legitimate business of government is to do for a people or a community those things which they cannot do at all for themselves, or cannot so well do in their separate capacities; but in all those things that people can do for themselves, the government ought not to interfere."

I think no better philosophy for a free government has ever yet been stated.

Now, Americans wanted a strong national defense at less cost. We have today the strongest armed forces of our peacetime history. In building them we have saved vast funds. We have cut red tape and eliminated duplication and waste. And let me make this clear: our military strength does not consist of forcibly recalled veterans who have already served our nation in war.

But, of course, our people also wanted a strong peacetime economy. For this, the Congress took many steps. It passed, for example, a new housing program. It passed an expanded highway program. It passed a new farm program to stop the seven-year decline in farmers' income—a program to promote lasting farm prosperity in an America no longer at war. And that program was designed also to remove the great surpluses that were breaking the back of the program then existing.

The Congress extended old age and survivors insurance to 10.2 million more Americans, and raised their benefits. And at last, my friends, these benefits include farmers who have been indirectly helping to pay the cost of the social security system all these years. The Congress extended coverage of unemployment compensation to 4 million more Americans. It passed tax revisions to encourage small business, and to eliminate inequities in the law.

Due to these and other measures, we have at last an economy whose strength is not sapped by the virus of inflation. It is an economy that doesn't compel the piling up of debts for our children—an economy whose strength is not dependent upon the sacrifices of the battlefield.

Without the economic collapse so widely forecast by professional pessimists, our nation has moved from war to peace.

Nevertheless, I am keenly aware that in some American localities, dislocations and hardships do exist. These are the inescapable aftermath of war and inflation. These problems we are striving constantly to ease. In the localities concerned, as well as in the rest of the country, we are taking concrete action to foster strength in the whole economy.

There was something else, two years ago, that all of us especially wanted. We wanted subversives out of the government service.

This Administration and the Congress are dealing decisively with the Communist menace. Supported by eleven new laws, we are backing to the hilt the Department of Justice and the FBI. There is no vacillation nor inaction on the part of this Administration in dealing with those who, by force or violence, would overthrow the government of the United States.

And abroad, we have an honest, forthright foreign policy concerned with deeds, not merely words. Over the globe our friends know our devotion to freedom. They know that America joins with those who help themselves in the effort to preserve liberty and peace.

Two years ago, war was raging in Korea and Indo-China. All Asia lay exposed to the steady advance of the Reds. Iran, with 60 per cent of the world's known petroleum reserves, was in deadly danger. Suez and Trieste posed constant threats to peace in the West. Europe had foundered on century-old differences, unable to build a position of reliable strength. Even in the Western Hemisphere, Communist imperialism had ominously appeared.

You know of the events that have since occurred.

In London, a few days ago, an agreement of momentous significance was signed that can powerfully strengthen the defenses of the West. Just this week, after almost a decade of anxious effort, Yugoslavia and Italy, with the encouragement and help of the Western world, settled their differences over Trieste.

For the first time in twenty years, there is no active battlefield anywhere in the world.

And, at last, we are harnessing the atom to the work of peace.

As for nations which, despite our best efforts, are still unfriendly, they harbor no delusions about the determination and the growing strength of the free world.

Recently, Communist imperialism discovered that the entire Association of American Republics means business in defending freedom. First at Caracas, then in ten short, determined days, the Communist beachhead in Guatemala was eliminated.

In all these ways, then, there has been progress of the most tremendous import to the peace and security of the Western world. Much of this progress is due to the richness of experience, imagination and determination of our distinguished Secretary of State. He and his colleagues in the State Department and the Foreign Service are carrying American prestige to new heights in foreign chancelleries.

Fellow citizens, I have recited some of the advances made in many fields in a short twenty months. For the most part, they have grown out of a cordial partnership between the Administration and the Congress. This cordiality has been a welcome relief from the bickering and the suspicion that for so long poisoned relations between the executive and legislative branches. In laws passed, and in heightened respect for their government, this harmony has brought immense benefits to the American people.

And now, let's take a quick look at the future.

Many things need to be done.

We must continue to foster the growth of a free economy to provide more jobs and higher living standards.

We must continue our efforts to cut the cost of government, so we can cut taxes still more.

We must continue each year to improve our peacetime farm program.

We must have a vast new highway program.

We must expand our foreign trade and American investment abroad. We must expand markets for America's farms and factories, if we are to keep prosperity within our own land.

We must write into law a national water resources program.

We must help our people meet their critical health and medical needs, while repudiating socialization of medicine.

We must find ways to encourage communities to provide the schoolhouses they need, and to improve opportunities for their schoolteachers.

We must build a new and effective reserve program for our armed forces.

We must begin to unravel the confused relations between the Federal, state and local governments, and make still more improvements in the organization of the Federal Government.

We must drive through partisan obstructions to achieve statehood for Hawaii, to lower the voting age in Federal elections, and to make our promised changes in the labor-management laws.

We must continue our historic advances in the vital area of civil rights.

We must vigorously push all constructive measures for promoting world peace, always strong and secure, but always fair and conciliatory.

Now, my friends, a cold war of partisan politics between the Congress and the executive branch won't give us these goals.

And this brings up a political fact of life.

You know perfectly well that you just can't have one car with two drivers at the steering wheel and expect to end up any place but in the ditch—especially when the drivers are set on going in different directions. By the same token, you cannot have efficient Federal government when the Congress wants to follow one philosophy of government and the executive branch another.

In our system of government, progress is made when the leaders of the executive branch and the majority of the Congress are members of the same political party. The unsurpassed record of the Eighty-third Congress is shining evidence of this truth. Moreover, in no other way can Americans hold one party and one group of people responsible either for success or lack of success.

History shows that when the executive and legislative branches are politically in conflict, politics in Washington runs riot. In these conditions, the public good goes begging while politics is played for politics' sake. Meanwhile, in the eyes of the world, we appear divided in council and uncertain in purpose.

These are the reasons—the compelling reasons—why the completion of your great program requires the election of a Republican-led Congress.

In our effort to keep the kind of government we want, you citizens are on the political front lines—the precincts of America. There you are as much a part of government as the sincere, hard-working men and women in Washington today who are trying to give you the kind of government you want.

As leaders and workers in your precincts, you know that the members of our party cannot carry this battle alone. We must enlist the spirited support of friends and neighbors, regardless of party, who believe in the same principles and objectives. Happily, we have been blessed with millions of such sturdy allies. For the cause in which we believe is bigger than any political party. To this cause, all Americans, regardless of party, can give their enthusiastic support.

And in this struggle, I know you will have the same determination—the same enthusiasm—the same drive—as you had two years ago.

For only through your effort can our program continue to advance.

Only through your effort will we continue to have the kind of America all of us so earnestly desire.

Together, my friends, we shall forge ahead in this great work we have so well begun, determined to keep America strong and secure—determined that this land of freedom, under Almighty God, will not rest until we see in the world a lasting peace with justice. Together we shall forge ahead to build in our America a steadily growing prosperity and happiness that will bring an ever brighter future for our people and for those who, after we are gone, must carry forward the banner of freedom.

That, my fellow Americans, is our kind of America.

Working together with those millions who have made common cause with us in this effort, that is the kind of America we shall have.

Thank you—thank you—and good night to all of you.

VOTE DEMOCRATIC [4]

PAUL H. DOUGLAS [5]

Senator Paul Douglas, up for reelection in Illinois, gave this address before the Citizens for Douglas Conference, at the Palmer House, Chicago on Saturday evening, September 25, 1954.

The Republican candidate, Joseph T. Meek, had been for twenty years a retail merchants' lobbyist (*Time,* October 15, 1954, p 15). He had the strong backing of the late Colonel Robert McCormick and his Chicago *Tribune,* Republican Senator Everett Dirksen, and the thousands of conservative Republicans of that state.

Senator Douglas, by contrast, before his election in 1948, had been professor of economics at the University of Chicago, a nationally known economist, and a reform member of Chicago's City Council. At the age of fifty he had been a World War II Marine. In the Senate itself he had emerged as the leader of a band of Democrats who fought vigorously and successfully against the Taft-Hoover thesis of semi-isolationism in the troubled world of 1950-51. The main lines of foreign policy Douglas supported were being carried out by Truman after 1952 and later by Eisenhower.

In the Illinois campaign of 1954 each senatorial candidate campaigned with tremendous energy, up and down the state "on both sides of the street." Personally each met as many of the 7.8 million citizens as possible, addressed meetings for almost fifteen hours on many a day, broadcast repeatedly by radio and television, and always was moving by auto from one end of the state to the other.

The political philosophies, personalities, and speaking techniques and platform mannerisms of the two differed widely. Mr. Meek referred to Senator Douglas as "the Professor from the Midway," and the "Senior Socialist Senator from Illinois." Senator Douglas in the Palmer House speech summarized Mr. Meek's position on major issues. Earlier the Republican candidate had been cool to President Eisenhower—ready to support him "when he is right." Later in the campaign Mr. Meek declared that his—Meek's—was "an Eisenhower campaign."

Senator Douglas called his opponent "the Republican Rip Van Winkle who has slept for twenty years in Lobbyland," "a man who was dragged screaming into the twentieth century."

The Douglas address printed below was highly personal—with some fifty "I's." He emphasized here the main issues that he preached from

[4] Text supplied by the "Citizens for Douglas Committee."

[5] For biographical note, *see* Appendix.

September to November, such as more decisive action to deal with un-employment ("280,000 in Illinois").

His arguments prevailed with the independents of Illinois and enough Republicans to give him the victory by a majority of some 250,000.[6]

My fellow citizens of Illinois:

We meet together tonight with the Citizens for Douglas, a group of citizens—independents, Democrats and Republicans —who are not working for me personally, but who are working for the principles of good government.

They are striving for the things in which they deeply be-lieve—for world peace through cooperation with our allies, for social progress and for the protection of the people's interest. I am greatly encouraged by their endorsement, and I am deeply grateful for their self-sacrificing work.

Individually, we may differ on an occasional issue. They know that my stands and my efforts cannot possibly follow any doctrinaire line. I believe in the two-party system. But in the final analysis, the judgment of any good citizen on all questions must be made from his inner convictions. That is what I have done. That is what I shall continue to do.

I believe that is what the people of Illinois wanted when, in 1948, you elected me your United States Senator. It seemed almost a hopeless campaign when we began. But with your help, what a tide it finally rolled up! It was a victory for a program and a set of ideals—won by the joint efforts of Re-publicans, Democrats and independents, farmers, workingmen and businessmen, who put these principles above all party con-siderations.

Personally, I am a Democrat and I am proud of it. But my decisions come from my own conscience, regardless of which party controls the national administration.

Here, then, is a summary of my record, on which the voters will pass this fall.

I have worked to cut wasteful government spending during the administrations of both political parties. With the splendid

[6] For further comment on Senator Douglas as a speaker, see his addresses with introductory notes in *Representative American Speeches: 1948-49*, p 179-95; *1950-51*, p72-4, 103-8; *1951-52*, p85-90.

support of Illinois citizens, I succeeded in saving the taxpayers over a billion dollars. Economy and efficiency in governmental operations are my constant watchwords—to squeeze out the fat without harm to our national defense, social services, veterans' benefits, and other essential programs.

If waste is nonpartisan, so is corruption. Thus I have also helped to expose favoritism and fraud in both administrations. Knowing that we cannot rely on mere exposure, however, I have also proposed remedies to prevent such misdeeds from occurring in the future.

Despite disagreements at times with the leadership in both political parties, I have worked for a stable economy, to avoid inflation when that was the danger, and recession now that this has become the problem.

In 1949 I helped to redraft and pass the Taft-Ellender-Wagner housing bill, and I have consistently fought ever since for slum-clearance and low-rent housing. I have worked for extended coverage and increased payments for old-age benefits and unemployment compensation, and I have sponsored successful bills to improve the railroad retirement act. I have sponsored bills aimed at achieving full employment.

I have fought monopoly by working to defeat the attempt of the gas industry to escape federal regulation, by opposing the monopolistic basing point system of fixing steel prices, and by helping to save for merchants the legitimate protections of the Robinson-Patman Act.

I have sought to reform congressional investigation procedures to conform them to elementary principles of justice and fair play.

I have always fought for rural electrification to improve conditions on the farm, and this last session, I helped win more adequate REA loan authorizations.

I have sponsored fair employment legislation and many other measures to establish equality of opportunity among all our citizens. For I believe with Lincoln, that in the face of life, we should lift the weights from the shoulders of all men.

In the field of foreign relations, I have recognized the terrible threat of aggressive communism and have favored programs to protect our national security, freedom and peace. I have given with deep conviction support to a stronger military defense, co-operation with the free nations, foreign military aid, expanded foreign trade, meeting human needs through economic assistance in underdeveloped areas, and an end to colonialism.

I am firmly committed to the principle of international co-operation—to the objective of collective security. There is no hope of peace or security without it. Isolation is the road to war and destruction. And the United Nations is the best available instrument for the peace-loving nations to reach their goal. We must strengthen, not weaken, it in all its branches.

Now, more than ever, there is a danger that we may be separated from our allies by forces seeking to divide us. This we cannot permit. I know the terrible costs of war. I know the ruthless destruction of tyranny. We must act together to prevent them both.

That is the general background of my record against which the more immediate issues of the last Congress and of this election are set.

Now, what about the present Administration under President Eisenhower? He is the Chief Executive of the United States. As a senator, my job is to evaluate the program he presents to the Congress and seek to protect the interests of Illinois and our nation to the best of my ability.

I am for the President's program when I conscientiously believe it is right. And I am against it when I believe it to be wrong.

I favor the main lines of the President's foreign policy and the progressive features of his domestic policy. Thus, despite confusing and conflicting statements by some Republican leaders, I have wholeheartedly supported the President's measures for bolstering the collective security of the free world. I have backed the military and economic assistance programs, and our continuing participation in the United Nations. I have voted for appropriations requested by the President to maintain our own defense strength. I favored his efforts to bring Germany into the Western European defensive coalition, to erect stronger international barriers against aggression in Southeast Asia, and the reciprocal trade agreement program largely scuttled by a section of the President's own party.

While I wished the Administration might have gone further, I have also fought for the President's public housing program, and his proposals to stimulate private housing construction. I have wholeheartedly backed the improvements he suggested in social security, unemployment compensation, vocational rehabilitation and the health reinsurance plan he sent to Congress.

Now let me mention frankly the record of my differences from his policies. I have opposed the give-away—take-away policies of the Republican Administration. I think the President was sold a bill of goods here.

I opposed with all my vigor the giving away of eight to fifty billion dollars' worth of offshore oil which belonged to all of us. Instead of giving it away to four coastal states, I tried to have these resources devoted to the education of our children in all the states, including Illinois.

I opposed the atomic energy bill of the Republican Administration because it turned over a $12 billion taxpayers' investment to the private power interests without adequate protection against monopoly and unwarranted high pices. I believe that the private utilities should also develop atomic energy uses, but not without protection for the consumers and taxpayers, generally.

I opposed the Administration's tax policies. They were against excise tax reductions—those on home appliances, railroad, airplane and bus fares, telephone service, and the like. I favored such tax cuts as aid to national economy, and we in Congress were successful in getting many reductions made.

The Administration also put over a big, general tax bill this year. There were some helpful reductions to a few who needed them. I supported those cuts which, however, amounted to only about an eighth of the total tax benefits. The remaining seven-eighths went mainly to American corporations and their stockholders.

Moreover, for the first time in American history, it was provided that income from stock dividends shall be taxed at a lower rate than earned income from labor, services, and other sources.

Instead of special concessions to stockholders which will mainly benefit only one per cent of American families, some of us wanted to have the general income tax exemption raised from $600 a person to $700 or $800. This would have saved the average family from $80 to $160 a year in taxes. This would have given relief to those who need it most, and would have been a more effective method of stimulating buying power and hence production and employment.

I did not agree with the Administration policies of reducing farm income by lower price supports. Farm income has fallen 15 per cent in the last two years, and should not be driven any lower.

I opposed the Administration's proposal to spend from $1 billion to $5 billion for irrigation on the upper Colorado River as waste of money. This is to provide irrigation for land at a cost of from $1,000 to $2,500 an acre. And when the money is spent and water put on the land, the improved land will be worth only about $150 an acre. Compare this with the price of the richest Illinois farm land of $500 to $600 an acre. This is the richest in the world.

In addition, the project would utterly destroy one of our finest national parks—Dinosaur National Monument.

I believe that the Federal Government should, instead, turn its attention to drought control in the great Midwest, where conditions are really serious.

This, then, is my position. You know how I stand in general and also in relation to the Eisenhower program. I favor, or oppose, the Administration on the basis of the merits of each issue, not personalities or party lines.

On November 2, we Americans will again exercise our right of free choice. What is the choice in Illinois this fall? You know who I am and what I stand for. My record is clean. But I have an opponent whose program you must consider also.

Early this year, the Republican party in Illinois had a primary to determine who should be my opponent. The race eventually narrowed down to eight candidates. So far as I know, all had commendable personal qualities.

There were, however, sharp differences of opinion among them. Some favored the President's program. Others opposed the President on his foreign policy and the progressive features of his domestic policies.

The man who became my opponent belongs to the latter group.

I do not deny his right to differ from the President, and I am hopeful that he will explain frankly where and why he does so as I have tried to do tonight and earlier. But it is important for the voters to know what those differences are, especially since he belongs to the President's own political party.

He favored the Bricker amendment—the President was against it. He called our allies "ingrate nations"—the President calls them friends. He has opposed the reciprocal trade and foreign aid programs—the President is for them. He has suggested that we walk alone—the President has urged greater allied cooperation.

He has attacked as "socialistic" virtually every progressive program favored by the President.

Let me give you some examples of programs he has called "socialism" or "peaceful communism," as reported in the Chicago *Daily News* of July 23:

Insurance of bank deposits
Guarantee of mortgages
Price supports for farm products
Agricultural credits
Social security systems
Veterans' benefits
New tariff regulations
Government-organized foreign loans
Public housing

Does this list shock you? It shocks me. I don't believe for a minute that it is "socialistic" for the government to protect your bank deposits or to pay social security benefits. I don't believe for a minute that any American citizen who believes in good government, who believes in government that is responsive to the needs of the people, is going to be bamboozled into thinking that this is "socialism." This is, rather—since my opponent appears not to understand—this is American democracy, democracy at its best, at work.

I do indeed favor those government programs. So do President Eisenhower and many Republicans. At least now that my opponent has attacked them as "socialistic," the issue between us is clear.

The decision in Illinois this fall will turn not alone on the regular political party organizations, as essential as these are. It will also turn on the individual citizens and organized, nonpartisan groups like yours, the Citizens for Douglas.

My friends, democracy is not a self-operating political system. It requires the best efforts of informed and active citizens. Our form of government, the democratic form of government, is one which really cares about the people. In turn, democracy itself demands, indeed it depends upon, the care and devotion of the people. It cannot exist, it cannot survive, without the thoughtful devotion of us all.

In answering the call of active citizenship, you—and many like you across the country—are not only advancing worthy immediate programs. You are also strengthening the enduring values which give life its meaning and purpose.

I have done my best for Illinois in the Senate and shall continue on the same path. You know my approach to issues. You know my policies. I stand on my record; you know my convictions and therefore you know the manner in which I will serve and represent you and our state.

Together, we shall strive for peace and justice in the world, and for equal rights and prosperity at home.

Together we shall go forward with our great work.

VOTE REPUBLICAN [7]

RICHARD M. NIXON [8]

Vice President Nixon broadcast this election eve appeal on November 1, 1954, to the voters of Denver, Colorado, over the Columbia radio and television system. At the conclusion of his half-hour speech, he introduced President Eisenhower, who, from the television studio in Washington, D.C., followed with a fifteen-minute talk.

Nixon's address, in contrast to his vigorous "cannonading" of the previous weeks, was aimed at all voters—to decide at the polls "what is best for America." His arguments, nevertheless, turned out to be an urgent drive for support of all Republican nominees.

His speech was on the whole toned down from the extreme claims and indictments of his September-October speechmaking. His address at Denver was an excellent example of persuasion. He developed the attention, need, satisfaction and action steps in regular order—as any good salesman would do. His motive appeals emphasized: (1) peace and security, (2) economic well being, (3) social and personal satisfaction, (4) assured defense against outside foes (communism), and (5) confidence in the great leader Eisenhower. The concreteness of detail and the vividness of language contributed to this persuasiveness. The delivery, too, was well adapted to the radio-television audience. Mr. Nixon's personality was well communicated to his listeners and viewers. Those who had previously admired him were no doubt further strengthened in their confidence in him. His opponents no doubt saw in him what they regarded as showmanship that aimed to win political battles at any costs.

Much speculation concerning Mr. Nixon's power as a campaigner followed the November vote. Oregon, Democratic in spite of Nixon's extended speaking there, was cited as an illustration of his inadequate political oratory. On the other hand, his speechmaking that covered most of the northern pivotal states was analyzed as an important reason for the slightness of the edge given to the Democrats in the voting. On the whole his prestige was not diminished in spite of his aggressive political speeches. In 1955 he was often mentioned as a fit running mate for President Eisenhower in 1956.[9]

[7] Text as recorded by the New York *Times*, November 2, 1954.

[8] For biographical note, see Appendix.

[9] For further comment on Vice President Nixon as a speaker, see *Representative American Speeches: 1952-53*, p72-82.

I want to say at the outset that I share the disappointment that I know millions of the fans of Lucille Ball and Desi Arnaz must feel at not getting to see their favorite show on this channel tonight. I'd like to be seeing it, too.

But tomorow, as all of you know, America must make a vital decision. It will affect the future of our people, of our children, for years to come. And I know that they—as well as you—would not want to miss this opportunity to hear from the President of the United States as you will in just a few moments.

But before the controls shift to Washington, I should like to talk to you tonight briefly on the issues of this campaign.

This will be a political talk such as you have probably never heard before.

Usually in political talks, the person who is asking for the support of candidates asks for it on one basis or another. Sometime he says vote for a man because you like him personally. And other times he says vote for him because he's a member of your own party.

I don't believe that either of these reasons is a good enough reason to support a man or a woman for public office, particularly during these very, very critical years.

I think that sometimes we kind of get fed up in America with the political cannonading that goes on during a political campaign. And I think that we like to consider in the quiet of our homes a very simple question—particularly on the day before election.

The question is: "What is best for America?" Not what is best for the candidate, not what is best for our party.

Not what is best for the candidate. Not what is best for our party. But what is best for America.

And so I'd like to talk tonight on that particular subject, because I'm prejudiced. I'm part of the Eisenhower Administration. I think that the Eisenhower Administration and the Republican Congress which the President has requested be elected will be in the best interests of the American people.

But let us test tonight that Administration against what Americans want from their Government. What is the major responsibility that a Government has?

Ask any mother with sons of draft age—she'll tell you. Keep the peace. Certainly nothing is more important than that. And I think that, as all of us realize, a hydrogen bomb can obliterate a city.

That there is nothing more important than to develop policies which will keep the peace and keep it without surrender. Because we can find solutions to all of our other problems, we can have the best social security program or unemployment compensation, or what have you, and it isn't going to do us any good unless we're around to enjoy those solutions.

And so, on this issue of whether or not the Administration is best qualified to keep the peace, let us test the Eisenhower leadership and the Eisenhower policies.

First, let's go back to 1952. Why did the American people believe that they needed a new leadership in the field of foreign policy in 1952? Because they realized that in seven years in which the previous Administration's policy had been in effect in America, that 600 million people had been lost to the Communist world.

The previous Administration policy was not all wrong, of course. It was right in recognizing the danger of communism in Europe.

But it was wrong in failing to estimate properly the danger of communism in Asia. And the result was the loss of almost a third of all the peoples of the world to the Communist conspiracy.

In addition to that, the Administration's policies had resulted in a war, a war in Korea that had cost us 140,000 American boys as casualties.

Do you recall what concerned the American people, however, about that war? It wasn't so much the fact that the war was going on, but it was the fact that this was a war we weren't allowed to win or end.

You remember the news reports. Up and down that dreary peninsula casualties every day and so the American people sensed that some way they needed new leadership, better leadership than they had. And they sensed also that in President Eisenhower they would get it.

Do you remember what he said at Detroit just a week before the election? Very simply he said: "I will go to Korea." He didn't make any promise that there was an easy answer, but the American people sensed from the way that he said it and from his past experience in leadership that here was a man.

Here was a man that could find a way to end this war and to keep America out of other wars like it.

So he was elected and he went to Korea, and twenty months have passed. And what is the result of his policy? Well, I say it's a great dramatic achievement which is summed up in a simple sentence: The war in Korea is over, and for the first time in fifteen years the world is at peace.

But there are other achievements, too. We found when we came to Washington in January 1953, that there were other hot spots in the world: in Suez, in Iran, in Trieste, in Indo-China, in Guatemala—any one of which might have flamed into war. But as a result of the diplomacy that we've had and the leadership that we have had those hot spots have been cooled off and no war has resulted.

In addition to that, may I say that people often ask the question, What is the policy that this Administration has? Why has it succeeded? And my answer is this:

First of all it's based on keeping America strong, at home militarily with just as many strong allies as we can get abroad. And may I say that today you can be confident that the United States and its allies are stronger than they've been at any time since World War II, and strong enough to resist the threat of Communist aggression any place in the world.

And secondly we recognize that our policy must be firm diplomatically. You can't be inconsistent in dealing with the international gangsters in Moscow and Peking.

And under Secretary of State Dulles and President Eisenhower we have this firm diplomacy—firm diplomacy that was capped by the agreement in Paris. Some of you may have seen Secretary of State Dulles report on it on television last Monday. One of the greatest achievements and victories in diplomacy that has ever been scored by an American secretary of state.

But, third, may I tell you also that there is another ingredient of success for a foreign policy to keep the peace. It may be the most important of all. You know what it is? Leaders who are cool in a crisis.

Let me tell you something. I sit in the high councils of this Administration. There have been occasions during the past twenty months when men who were unwise, men who were impulsive might have plunged the United States into war. But because in the President, in the Secretary of State we had men of judgment and background the United States has not only been gotten out of one war, we had been kept out of others.

Oh, I know some of the critics say the policy is a failure—but what is the test of success or failure of foreign policy? It's whether it keeps the peace. The previous policy got the United States into war. The Eisenhower policy got us out of war.

And I say that the men best qualified to keep the peace in the future are those who got us out of war, who kept us out of others, and whose leadership has made it possible for us to say tonight that the chances for peace in our time, and in the time to come, are brighter tonight than they had been at any time since World War II.

And so on this issue, I say, whether you're a Democrat or a Republican, President Eisenhower deserves the support of the American people. He deserves the Republican House and Senate that he has asked the people to elect.

And what else do the American people want from their Government, besides peace?

Well, putting it very simply, they want prosperity but, getting right down to brass tacks, they want a kind of a policy that will allow them to meet the bills at the end of the month—good jobs, good pay, security against old age, progress for the future.

Now, how does this Administration measure up on this issue?

Again, let's go back to January 1953, when we came to Washington. We found that the previous Administration's policies—the same type of policies—had been in effect for twenty years in America. Now what were they? They were high taxes, high spending, controls on the economy and inflation.

Now in that twenty-year period we found, however, that that type of policy had never brought prosperity to America except when we had a war. Let me give you the proof.

In 1940, the last peacetime year before World War II, there were 10 million unemployed in America, four times more than there are today.

In 1949, the last peacetime year before Korea, there were 5.5 million unemployed in America. That's twice as many as there are today.

So what does that indicate? It means that that type of policies cannot bring prosperity in peacetime; we need some other type.

And so this Administration has adopted a different kind of policies—and what are they? Just the opposite. We cut spending, we cut taxes, we took the controls off of the economy, we checked inflation.

What's the result?

This is the best peacetime year in America's history.

Employment is higher, unemployment is lower than in any peacetime year in the last quarter of a century. Wages and take-home pay are higher than they have been in any peacetime year in America's history. But most important of all, look what's happened to jobs. Since January of this year there have been 2.3 million new jobs created in America. That's why unemployment has gone down. This is why employment has gone up.

Now what kind of jobs are they? They are permanent, peacetime, wealth-creating jobs rather than temporary, wartime, wealth-destroying jobs.

Now how did they come about? Because the people who create jobs, who invest in businesses, who expand all businesses or invest in new businesses had confidence in this Administration.

Now let us see what would happen if we elected a Congress which had men in it who sincerely but nevertheless honestly believed in the type of economic policies which we had previously.

Well, just consider what you would do. Suppose you were going to invest in a new business. Suppose that you were going to expand an old business. Suppose that you were confronted with the Congress that you knew might raise your taxes, put controls on you, socialize maybe your particular kind of business, take it over by the Government? You know what you would do.

You would slow down.

So what does that mean? If we elect that kind of a Congress, this tremendous expansion that we have will be checked.

If we elect that kind of a Congress we run the risk that the new jobs won't be created which will keep up with America's growing working force.

And what does that mean? More unemployment.

Now, what is the Eisenhower program, the Eisenhower way? It is to continue these kinds of stable policies that I've mentioned, policies which will bring more investment in America's future.

But far more than that also, it means, it means that this Administration is not satisfied with things as they are. We believe in being progressive.

That's why we have the greatest highway program that America's ever seen on the books, coming for the future, $50 billion in ten years.

Think what that will do for the expansion of America. That's why we are developing America's water and power resources. But on a partnership basis with the states and local communities rather than every time the Federal Government helping out a local or state community proceeding on the theory that then it gets a right to set up a Federal colony run by bureaucrats from Washington, D.C.

And that is why the goal that we aim for, the one that President Eisenhower laid out on Monday of this week, ten years from now a gross national product of $500 billion, is possible provided we keep faith with the American system, provided we continue to support the Administration's policies.

So in this connection, if we want more jobs, if we want higher wages, if we want the real prosperity which is based on peace rather than on war, the way is the Eisenhower way. The way is a Republican House and Senate which shares his economic philosophy.

What else do we want? Well, of course, we want a lot of things, and I haven't time to discuss them all.

We want our Government to be liberal and humanitarian. And we're proud of the fact that this Government of ours is liberal and humanitarian. We've expanded social security, we've expanded unemployment insurance, we had programs in the field of health, and education and welfare. And what is the difference between our programs and those of our predecessors? A very simple one.

We think that it's possible to be liberal and humanitarian without being socialistic.

What else do we want? We want government which provides opportunity for our children—opportunity for our children regardless of their background, their race, their creed or their color. And may I say we're particularly proud tonight. This Administration has done so much to end discrimination and unemployment in America.

May I say that if we can continue our policies, that we feel that our policies—which are based not on demagoguery, not on compulsion—but on persuasion, upon education—that these policies will make the American dream come true—the dream of equal opportunity for all regardless of race or creed or color.

We want an Administration which is honest. And may I say in that connection that you can be sure that this Administration is honest. And it will remain honest just as long as President Eisenhower is President of the United States.

And, finally, we want our Government to be loyal. Why is this important? Not because there's any danger that the Communists are going to overthrow this Government in your, our time, or in the time to come, but because the major enemy of the United States—the international Communist conspiracy—has its tentacles all over the world right here in the United States.

And therefore you must deal with this conspiracy. And may I say that we have dealt with it. We've dealt with it fairly, sanely and effectively. Where our predecessors, unfortunately, not because of disloyalty, or lack of patriotism, but because of ignorance and blindness did not deal with it effectively.

What have we done? Well, we've enforced the laws on the books, we've removed security risks; we've gotten new laws—

new laws which make the penalty for treachery fit the crime in America.

I haven't time to discuss those laws, but just let me describe one of them. You may remember the President, in his state of union message asking the Congress to pass a bill that would take away the citizenship of anyone who participated in the conspiracy to overthrow the Government by force or violence. That bill is now law.

And I say it's a good law.

That bill is now law. And I say it's a good law because no one can travel through this country of ours as I have without realizing what a great and a good land this is and what a privilege it is to be an American citizen.

And I say that anybody who voluntarily joins the Communist conspiracy when he has the privilege of being an American, I say that when he does that that such an individual doesn't deserve to be an American citizen, and under the laws as passed now his citizenship will be taken away from him.

And so the sure way to continue this program which is smashing the Communist conspiracy to bits, I say, is to elect a Republican House and Senate who favor this program and who will not be sniping at it, who will not be cutting at it as some of the critics of the program have in the past few days and months.

Well, I believe this is a great record. And I know that to keep this record going, to continue this leadership, we need a Republican House and Senate—because it wouldn't have been possible to have gotten it through in the past twenty-two months unless we had a Republican House and Senate. It won't be possible unless we have it in the future.

Finally, may I just add this last word. What will you be voting for tomorrow if you vote for a Republican House and Senate that will support President Eisenhower?

You're going to be voting for government, in my opinion, which has the best chance to bring peace without surrender for America. The best chance to provide sound, solid prosperity without war. The best chance of government which is humanitarian and liberal without being socialistic, a government that is honest and loyal and decent.

This Government—this Administration—isn't perfect. We've made mistakes, and we will make some in the future. But I believe that this Eisenhower Administration has given America the best government that it's had in my lifetime.

And I believe if you study it as I have you will agree.

May I add just a last word. I'm often asked what kind of a man this President of ours is? I've gotten to know him very well over the past twenty-two months. I've seen him make very great decisions for America. And in making those decisions may I say that as I watched him and if you had watched him you would have even greater confidence than you presently have in the President of the United States, because no man could be more dedicated, no man could work harder, no man could believe more deeply in America than he does.

I am proud to be on his team. I believe that all of the American people should consider this as they go to the polls tomorrow.

And now, as I present him to you, may I just say this. Regardless of how we vote tomorrow, every American can be proud of the fact that he can hold the President of the United States up to his children as a man who has faith in God, faith in America, and who has restored real dignity and respect to the highest office in this land.

My fellow Americans, speaking to you from Washington, D.C., I present the President of the United States.

COOPER UNION ADDRESS [10]

ADLAI E. STEVENSON [11]

Adlai E. Stevenson gave this political address on Saturday night, October 30, 1954, before an overflow audience of 2,000 in the Great Hall of Cooper Union, New York City.

The occasion marked the climax of Mr. Stevenson's energetic and extensive campaign beginning in August for the election of Democratic governors, in this case, Averell Harriman of New York, and Democratic congressmen. Earlier in the day he had given stump speeches in Harlem and in Westchester County. On those occasions he had been at times in a lighter mood. In Harlem, for example, he had referred to the Republican charges that Mr. Harriman had been technically disqualified as a candidate for governor by reason of a vote two years previously in a Washington, D.C. presidential preference primary. "They are trying to disqualify Harriman because he voted, but they elected a President who had never voted."

Mr. Stevenson's address, as usual, was well organized, with its opening eulogy of Mr. Harriman; refutation, point by point, of the main theses of President Eisenhower in his recent Republican appeals; a climax of appeal for "healthy debate" and for the exercise of justice and conscience.

Republican critics were quick to denounce the speech. Said Leonard W. Hall, chairman of the Republican National Committee (as quoted by William S. White in the New York *Times* of November 1):

> We ran a check on this strange speech and found that in thirty minutes this spokesman for the Democrat left wing resorted to catastrophe-laden words no less than ninety-eight times.

> Mr. Stevenson used the word *division* or *divided* seven times, the word *confusion* six times, the word *peril* or *imperiled* three times, the word *mistrust* two times.

> In his almost hysterical stream of invective, Mr. Stevenson also used these words: *false, threatening, quicksands, slander, innuendo, demoralized, harried, alarming, degeneration, malice, baleful, fear* and *hate.*

> The one thing lacking from Mr. Stevenson's chatter was facts and constructive thoughts. Mindful of this, the voters will render both their literary and political judgment on this "three-scares-a-minute" speech at the polls tomorrow, just as they gave Mr. Stevenson their answer two years ago.

[10] The text is from the New York *Times*, Sunday, October 31, 1954.
[11] For biographical note, see Appendix.

On the next day, Mr. Stevenson received an honorary degree at the final convocation marking the celebration of Columbia University's two hundredth anniversary.[12] Said President Kirk of Columbia in citing Mr. Stevenson:

Man of politics, man of ideals; urbane graduate of a sister university which, in training him, served well the national community; entrusted on many occasions with high appointive office always administered with distinction; as governor of a great state, fully justifying the confidence of the electorate; as chosen leader of his national party, carrying his responsibilities with zeal and intelligence; a man of courage and a man of humility, an exemplar of the finest traditions of our public life.

On Monday night, November 1, Mr. Stevenson gave his final appeal out of Chicago to the nation over CBS-TV.

The election gave New York to Averell Harriman over Irving M. Ives; Illinois, to Paul Douglas over Joseph Meek; and a Democratic House, 232 to 203, and Senate, 48 to 47 (with Senator Morse supporting the Democrats there) in Washington.

Mr. Stevenson in 1954 well sustained his 1952 reputation for effective campaign speaking, especially in his radio-television appearances. Endorsed as he was by Averell Harriman and other successful candidates, Mr. Stevenson—if interested in a second try at the high office—was apparently well on the way to renomination in 1956.

As a son of Illinois I am a little awed to be speaking in Cooper Union, the scene of one of Abraham Lincoln's most famous speeches.

Tonight the campaign of 1954 is drawing to a close. Next Tuesday, as the tumult and the shouting die away, we shall go to the polls, as we have gone before, in a mood of solemnity and responsibility to register our decision. I hope that all of us will go, and that all of us will take counsel from conscience and intelligence as we cast our votes. For voting is, in a sense, a sacrament of our democratic way of life.

When we vote, we affirm our faith as free men and women in free government and society. And the survival of free government is what the contest of the mid-century and the clamor about Communists is all about.

This has been, in many respects, an interesting campaign. Our President has just completed an inspection of selected air-

[12] See below, p 123.

ports. And Vice President Nixon is finishing an extensive tour—
one might call it an ill-will tour. The Republican Cabinet has
been deployed in strategic points across the land.

And we Democrats have been busy, too. I have been proud
to speak on behalf of Democratic candidates here and there all
about the country and nowhere have I been prouder than here in
New York on behalf of the Democratic candidate for Governor,
whose distinguished and responsible career in the service of our
Government has few counterparts—Mr. Averell Harriman.

The story of Averell Harriman is the story of a notable
chapter in the diverse life of our democracy—of that small group
of American businessmen who were ahead of their time; who
recognized in the great depression a challenge not merely to our
economic system but to our system of freedom; who turned their
backs on the old deal and joined in the great constructive national
effort which saved not only business, but freedom itself; and
who ushered in what I like to describe—in contrast to our present
national frenzy—as twenty years of reason.

Now as this campaign approaches its end, I want to discuss
as soberly as I can what is at stake on Tuesday for all of us.

Let me first say very briefly why I think a Democratic Congress would be good for the country—indeed why it might even
be good for the Republican party.

Now it is both customary and fitting that the President should
desire and ask for a Congress of his own political persuasion,
for the President is also the leader of his party. But it is an
entirely different matter to say that the President is somehow
and in some way entitled to a Congress of his own choosing.
It is not the President but the people who choose the Congress;
and our biennial elections were specifically designed by the
founding fathers to provide the people this opportunity to
periodically record their judgment of an Administration.

I might add that I do not recall the Republicans ever advancing the argument that a President was entitled to a Congress
of his own party when there was a Democratic Administration
in Washington. Nor do I think it very likely that they will be
making this argument in, say, 1958.

He has said a Democratic Congress would mean a cold war between the Congress and the White House, but if we are to judge by the record of the last Republican Congress there can be no war colder, or hotter, than the internal conflict in the Republican party.

I need only remind you of the Bricker amendment; of Senator McCarthy's attack on the executive department; of incessant contradictions of the President's foreign policy by even the Republican majority leader, Senator Knowland, and of so many other conflicting voices that it has not been clear who speaks for America.

But on Thursday night General Eisenhower once again summarized his case for a Republican Congress by suggesting that—and I quote him—"confusion can be avoided and steady progress assured only by electing a Republican majority." I could hardly believe my eyes. Indeed I would like to use these words of the President as my own text. For I deeply believe that the only way to end the lamentable confusion of these last two years at home and abroad and the only way to resume confident steady social and economic progress is to elect a Democratic Congress.

Now let us consider foreign affairs. Our foreign policy, the level of our military strength, our system of alliances have been systematically imperiled by compromises, by contradictions and by appeasement of the Republican Old Guard.

Except, that is, when the Democrats have rescued the President from his own party and his own leadership. Democrats, for example, tried to resist the policy of reducing our national strength. Democrats tried to save President Eisenhower's own foreign trade program from the Republican protectionists. Democrats effected the confirmation of his Ambassador to Moscow against Republican opposition.

On twelve key Administration bills in foreign policy the Democrats not only provided the margin of victory, but on each one the Democrats actually gave the President more votes in both Senate and House than he received from his own party.

But the Democratic minority could not always save us from the Republican Old Guard.

When the President insists, as he did on Thursday, that his Administration has been more faithful to bipartisanship in foreign policy "than any previous Administration," one must charitably assume that he has been misinformed again. Under the Roosevelt and Truman Administration, dozens of leading Republicans shared in the responsibility for the formulation and execution of foreign policy—including General Eisenhower and Mr. Dulles, themselves. Where, I could respectfully ask the President, are the Democrats who play similar roles in his Administration? Where, even, are the Republicans who served under Democratic Administrations and have been dismissed to please the Old Guard?

Now either to please the Old Guard, or to get votes, the Administration embarked on a perilous course of foreign-policy-by slogan, by threat and by bluff. The reckless words about "liberation," about "atomic retaliation," about "seizing the initiative," while the Communists were seizing Indo-China, about "unleashing Chiang Kai-shek" and the like may have warmed the hearts of the Old Guard. But abroad they frightened our friends if not our enemies—whose aggressions and whose influence have steadily increased in the past two years.

Thanks to the Republican primitives, the Administration has muffled the Voice of America, has cut our Army, has scuttled our foreign trade program, has demoralized our foreign service; has intimidated and alarmed our allies and our unity of purpose has dissolved into the impotence of conflicting statements, conflicting policies and conflicting hopes. And, on every one of these issues, it was the Democrats in Congress who consistently stood for steadiness and for strength.

Now the President asks us to believe that all will be different in the next two years—that he can do with a Republican Congress what he couldn't do with a Republican Congress—that a Republican victory will somehow cause the Old Guard to change its spots and to reappear in the next Congress, purified and repentant. But I say that experience is the best teacher and that a Republican victory will not only give them new confidence and deepen the divisions in the Republican party but will imperil all of us.

And all this holds equally true for domestic policy as well. At first the Republicans laid claim to a record of legislative achievement. And latterly we've heard less about this record and more about Communists in government, about subversion and about sin. Probably this is because most of the positive accomplishments of the Administration were made possible only by Democratic votes. But I shall only mention the other parts that were put through without Democratic votes—in spite of Democratic opposition—for only those represent the distinctive contributions of this Administration and only those would be threatened by a Democratic Congress.

What has President Eisenhower sought in the domestic field against Democratic opposition?

Against Democratic opposition he put through a tax program in which the main benefits went overwhelmingly to the corporations and to stockholders.

Against Democratic opposition he has sponsored a wide and various give-away program. Ranging from public power development to grazing lands, from oil to Dixon-Yates, from atomic patents to water power sites, the Administration has not only reversed a bipartisan conservation policy of fifty years standing but has disclosed an alarming disposition to transfer our national possessions and resources from the many to the few.

Against Democratic opposition, the Administration has enacted a new farm program. As a matter of good faith in politics, it seems to me reprehensible that this program was enacted on a foundation of false pledges and of broken promises. But what is more important is that it means lower farm prices, with no corresponding decrease in sight for reductions in the cost of what the farmer has to buy.

I could go on. Only this week it was revealed that the Republican National Committee has become a recruiting agency for filling government jobs, even career jobs under Civil Service, which carries spoils politics back to the days that we hoped were gone forever.

But no situation at home is more disturbing than the fact that many, many of us seek work and cannot find it. The complacency of the Administration about unemployment and the economic decline, indeed the positive pride that the situation is no worse, has concerned many Americans for many months. Total output is down $14 million; one out of twenty Americans is out of work. Although the President said on last Monday—and I emphatically agree with him—that—and I quote him—"in our economy, to stand still is to fall behind," he still says—and I quote him again—"in the past two years there have been heartening events" and he speaks boastfully of "the most prosperous peacetime in our history."

But more disturbing still is that not just the Vice President and the Republican campaigners but now the President himself has affirmed the proposition that our prosperity has been achieved in the past only at the price of war and bloodshed. This of course has been standard Communist propaganda for years and is believed by many to prove that the United States is ready to precipitate war in order to save capitalism.

I am sure that the President must have spoken thoughtlessly and carelessly; and let me say to our friends and our enemies beyond the seas that no one who sincerely believes in free capitalism can believe that we can only be prosperous when at war.

Moreover the facts contradict it. The President evidently forgets the successful transition from war to peace in 1945 and 1946, when in a single year 8 million men were released from the armed services and defense spending fell ten times as much as in the past year. Yet in 1946, we had far less unemployment than we have today. One must assume, too, that the President has not been informed about the prosperous peacetime years of 1947 and 1948 when defense spending was less than one third as large as it is today, and yet unemployment was at least a million less. Of course, a Democratic Congress will not solve all our problems. But on a whole series of issues—defense, foreign policy, anti-depression, civil liberties—a Democratic Congress is more likely to bring about healthy results.

The election of a Democratic Congress on Tuesday will check the tendency of the last two years to separate the United States from our allies in world affairs. It will stem the drive to cut back further on our own armed strength. It will diminish the passion to give away our natural resources. It will stop further Dixon-Yates contracts. It will restore the dignity of the congressional investigation and will strengthen the atmosphere of individual freedom. It will chasten the Administration's complacent attitude toward the millions of Americans who cannot find jobs. It can do much to bring back intelligence, sobriety and purpose to the American government. And a Republican victory this fall can only confirm and intensify the tendencies which have brought us into such disrepute abroad and into such disunion at home.

And a Democratic victory will mean a gain for responsibility in another way—in a way perhaps more important than substantive issues at stake in the campaign. For the success of our democracy depends on the extent to which politics can serve the end of education, of justice and of truth. Those who would degrade our political processes threaten to destroy the very essence of a free system. If these methods succeed today then they will be used again and again, until freedom, dignity, decency themselves sink from sight into quicksands of confusion, mistrust and fear.

All thoughtful citizens have been concerned about the progressive degeneration of this present political campaign. We have observed with sorrow the effect that the pressures of partisanship and of political ambition have had upon the top leaders of the Republican party. When the campaign began, the President said that the only issue was the record of his Administration. But the end is a reckless campaign of smear, of misrepresentation and of mistrust. No reputation, no record, no name—no Democrat in short—has been immune from savage or sly attack on his integrity, his good sense, his very loyalty. A few days ago, when the President was asked what he thought of this kind of campaign in a press conference, he said he hadn't heard about it. But within twenty-four hours—and despite his earlier protestation that communism was not an issue in this campaign—he wrote Vice President Nixon expressing his gratitude and his admiration for Mr. Nixon's contribution to political enlightenment. And yesterday, if you please, in his airport tour the President himself found it in his heart, or in his script, to take up these themes himself.

But the great crusade ended a year ago, not this week. It ended a year ago when Mr. Brownell, President Eisenhower's Attorney General, impugned the very loyalty of President Truman, when Governor Dewey of New York identified all Democrats with death and with tragedy in Korea, when the Republican National Committee sent Senator McCarthy around the country to talk of twenty years of Democratic treason. Evidently the President couldn't control the campaign of slander, then, and evidently he has embraced it now.

I am sure that President Eisenhower could have accepted this strategy only because he has forgotten what I believe he really knows, and will once again remember—that how one wins in politics is as important as what one wins.

If ever our system should rise to the highest dignity of its tradition and its responsibilities, it is today. If ever we needed politics which would leave our people informed and united, not confused and divided, it is now. If ever smears, slander, innuendo, misrepresentation were out of place in our national life, it is in this time, at this place, in this world.

Our nation faces grim years ahead—years which will test to the utmost our resolution, our will and our faith. The realities of our existence—the severe and the menacing problems which hang over us—will be as harsh on the day after the election as they were the day the campaign began. After a responsible campaign, our country and our people would have been better equipped to cope with these realities than they were three months ago. Instead, the nation has been recklessly torn apart in the search for votes, with careless disregard for our self-respect, for our unity, for our national purpose, if you please.

The challenge is not just to win elections. The greater challenge is to live in pride and in freedom in a future so precarious and so threatening that we can risk no missteps and no miscalculations. We need to unite our country, not to divide it; to heal our wounds, not to enlarge them. The times demand, not mistrust and suspicion and fear, but more mutual respect and confidence and understanding than ever before.

This does not mean a suspension of hard and healthy debate, for hard and healthy debate is the essence of democracy. But hard and healthy debate has to do with real problems. It has to do with legitimate differences in policy and program. And I assure you that there is plenty in the realm of valid difference between our two parties to provide material for a dozen hard-fought political campaigns. No one needs to invent issues or to misrepresent them or to falsify them. No one needs to make confusion a policy and corruption a faith.

I say corruption, because this kind of campaign threatens to corrupt the very processes on which the functioning of democratic government depends. To say that one or another American lacks patriotism or favors communism or wants to subvert our freedom—when his only crime is the crime of disagreement—is to shake our system to the foundations. If we lose our faith in each other, we have lost everything; and no party victory is worth this. Those who seek victory at this price can be rebuked in only one way—that is, at the polls. And this, I think, is the deepest meaning and the greatest opportunity for the American voters on Tuesday.

I would plead with all Americans to cleanse their minds of suspicion and hate; to recognize that men may differ about issues without differing about their faith in America or their belief in freedom; that politics must be a means, not of compounding our weakness, but of consolidating our strength.

If we do justice on Tuesday to our own conscience and sense of responsibility, then alone can we do justice to the nation we love; then alone can we make our beloved nation a symbol and shrine of hope and faith for all free men.

LEGISLATIVE CENSURE

FOR CENSURE OF SENATOR McCARTHY [1]

John C. Stennis [2]

Senator John C. Stennis, Democrat of Mississippi, spoke before the United States Senate on November 12, 1954, in support of the resolution to censure Senator Joseph McCarthy.

Senator Stennis, a member of the Senate's special censure committee, indicted Senator McCarthy for his alleged continued abuse of the Senate.

The Senate had met in extraordinary session four days before to consider the report of the Select Committee appointed to study the censure charges.

The bipartisan six-man group, under chairman Senator Arthur Watkins, Utah Republican, was set up in August. On September 27 grounds for censure on two counts were presented: (1) Senator McCarthy had acted contemptuously toward a Senate subcommittee investigating charges against him involving his finances; (2) Senator McCarthy had used "reprehensible" language to Brigadier General Ralph Zwicker during hearings on the discharge of Major Irving Peress, an Army dentist accused of pro-communism. Behind these charges was the implication that his investigating methods, his denunciation of all who opposed him, his defiance of President Eisenhower's authority, brought into disrepute the United States Senate.

Although the debate was scheduled to begin on November 10, Senator McCarthy on November 9 released a long speech that he proposed to give before the Senate the next day. (He did not deliver it but inserted it in the *Record*.) Statements in that "speech" further inflamed some Senators.

Senator Watkins opened the debate. Senator McCarthy subjected him to long cross-examination. Senator Case of South Dakota, also on the Select Committee, suggested that if Senator McCarthy would apologize for charge number one both charges might be handled without censure.

In this atmosphere Senator Stennis spoke in ringing tones and with much physical aggressiveness before the crowded galleries and chamber. He made the issue not militancy against communism, as Senator McCarthy

[1] *Congressional Record.* 100:14857-60. November 12, 1954 (daily edition).
[2] For biographical note, see Appendix.

argued it should be, but McCarthyism—"political morality in senatorial conduct." Senator Bricker, among others, replied.[3]

On Monday, November 15, Senator Jenner led the debate for Senator McCarthy, and Senator Ervin, of North Carolina, called for censure. On November 16, Senators Watkins, Welker, and Case continued the debate, and Senator McCarthy entered the Naval Hospital at Bethesda, Maryland, with a disabled elbow. The Senate adjourned from November 18 until November 29.

On Thursday, December 2, after three days of debate and preliminary voting on resolutions to soften the resolution, the Senate voted 67 to 22 to "condemn" the Wisconsin Senator.

On January 20, 1955, the Senator lost his chairmanship of the Government Operations Committee and its Permanent Subcommittee on Investigations as a result of the 1954 elections, which returned a Democratic majority to the Senate. Speculation continued concerning his role as aggressive fighter against communistic subversion and as spokesman for Republican dissenters against Eisenhower.

Mr. President, what is the question here? It is purely a question of political morality in senatorial conduct. To be more precise, the question is whether I, as a senator, approve or disapprove of these proven acts as proper standards of senatorial conduct. Each senator must make up his own mind about what are the proper standards; but, as senators, let us remember that it is not as individuals that we are to make up our minds in this case. We are to make them up as representatives of the 161 million people of the United States; we are setting standards of conduct for a time-proven and time-tested institution which belongs to the people—the United States Senate. . . .

This is not merely a question of an attack upon a member of the committee. I would not pass it by if it were. But that is not all it was. As I recall, I am the member of the committee who said that the remarks of the junior Senator from Wisconsin with reference to Senator Hendrickson belong in the category relating to the treatment of the committee, because the senator from New Jersey was a member of that committee, and the insult to him was not merely an insult to an individual. It was an insult to the constituted authority of the Senate, which was carrying out a constitutional mission. Moreover, there was an insult to a constitutional authority, the personnel of which had recently

3 See below, p 113-22.

been expressly approved, including Senator Hendrickson, by a unanimous vote of the Senate.

Is it a sufficient answer to say, "Joe has done some good in hunting Communists"? Shall we destroy what have been considered the necessary processes in carrying out one mission because a man has done good in another field, on another mission? I cannot assent to such an argument.

In view of the facts which I have related, do senators believe that the mission of the subcommittee was obstructed? Do senators think there was an obstruction of justice? Of course, they do. There is no way to avoid such a conclusion. That is the final reason why I say there is no escape from an affirmative charge. Such conduct must be condemned. Otherwise, when challenge is made of these facts, and we fail to disapprove them, we adopt them as a standard. Let us be clear. Let us tell the youth of this country, "This is the way. This is the high road of which the Senate approves, and upon which it likes to travel in the consideration of public business." That is the conclusion of this member of the committee.

That is not all. After the report was filed and the subject set for special consideration by the Senate, and after the Senate had reassembled, the first words to be uttered on the floor by this same source of conduct were a continuation of the slush and the slime which have been poured on other committees which were charged with the duty of trying to look into the conduct. I have no personal resentment toward the junior Senator from Wisconsin for having made such statements. I feel sorry for him for having done so. I refer to Senator McCarthy's speech which was not delivered on the floor, but released to the press and inserted in the *Congressional Record* on the first day of the debate. It represented a continuation of the same pattern, his same course of conduct. It is another spot on the escutcheon of the Senate, another splash and splatter.

Every senator must decide this case for himself. As for the senator from Mississippi, I cannot approve such slush and slime as a proper standard of senatorial conduct as we labor to carry on and transact the business of the people. For that reason, and that reason alone, I state my position here.

I repeat that the question before the Senate is not a question of fact. The facts are agreed upon. The question is not, "Do we approve or disapprove of everything that was done or everything that was said by every member of the committee at every turn throughout these proceedings?" The question is one purely of political morality in senatorial conduct. To be precise, the question is, "As a senator, and not merely as an individual, do I approve or do I disapprove of these proven facts as proper standards of senatorial conduct?"

If we approve, then something big and fine will have gone from this chamber and something wrong, something representing a wrong course, will have entered and gotten itself accepted as a proper standard of conduct.

As we consider that question, I hope that in some way each senator will seek and finally find divine guidance in deciding what his duty is, and, from the same source, find help and encouragement in performing that duty.

Mr. President, I yield the floor.

AGAINST CENSURE OF SENATOR McCARTHY

JOHN W. BRICKER [5]

Senator John W. Bricker, Republican of Ohio, gave this lengthy argument before the United States Senate, on November 12, 1954, in opposition to the resolution of censure of Senator Joseph McCarthy.

Senator Stennis, who opened the day's debate [6] was sharply cross-examined by Senator McCarthy. Senator Bricker followed and with a defense of the junior Senator from Wisconsin not so much on personal as on legal grounds. According to Senator Bricker, the censure in this case would not furnish a precedent for similar cases of censure for similar free usages of language. The result would be legislative tyranny. The rules of the Senate provide no punishment for acts here charged as offenses. Obviously, is the standard of conduct imposed by the resolution against the junior Senator from Wisconsin to be therefore applied impartially to all present and future senators? "No!" was Senator Bricker's answer.

The final vote, on December 2, was 67 for and 22 against the resolution. Senator Bricker, absent, was paired with Senator Albert Gore of Tennessee. ("If present the Senator from Ohio would have voted 'Nay.' ") Other members of the minority group, all Republicans, were Senators Styles Bridges of New Hampshire, Everett Dirksen of Illinois, Henry C. Dworshak of Idaho, Bourke Hickenlooper of Iowa, W. E. Jenner of Indiana, W. F. Knowland of California, Herman Welker of Idaho.[7]

Mr. President, I wish to speak very briefly this afternoon about the matter which is before the Senate.

I oppose the resolution to censure the junior Senator from Wisconsin.

If censure is voted in this case, it is highly improbable that other senators would be censured for comparable acts. The result of censure, therefore, would be one so close to legislative tyranny that I cannot view it with complacency.

[4] *Congressional Record.* 100:14869-72. November 12, 1954 (daily edition).

[5] For biographical note, see Appendix.

[6] See above, p 109-12.

[7] For further comment on Senator Bricker as speaker, see *Representative American Speeches.* 1953-54, p75-80.

Fortunately, we are not all of the same mold. Every senator should be free to do his job in his own way, so long as he acts within the law and within the rules of the Senate.

The framers of the Constitution faced the problem of legislative tyranny. They limited the powers of Congress to those specifically delegated by the Constitution. Two forms of legislative tyranny were specifically prohibited—ex post facto legislation and bills of attainder. To the Founding Fathers, therefore, legislative tyranny seemed just as ugly as the tyranny of the despot or of a mob.

In this case, the Senate is sitting as judge, prosecutor, and jury. However, I do not suggest, nor do I intend to imply even remotely, that the Senate of the United States is imbued with the spirit of punitive action. I yield to no man in the respect I hold for the processes and traditions of this body. Nevertheless, if the consequence of Senate action is to single out one senator for punishment and to excuse all others liable to punishment on the same basis, the result is an injustice.

Unjust punishment is that having no basis in any rule of law. The victim may receive an eminently fair trial. But if his punishment is based on ex post facto legislation, or on no law at all, he is truly the victim of injustice.

No punishment can be just if it is not based on any law that is known, knowable, or predictable. We are not concerned here with the problem of power. A mob has power, unlawful power to be sure. The Senate of the United States in this proceeding is armed with constitutional power. Article I, section 5 of the Constitution provides that "each House may punish its Members for disorderly behavior." But unless the exercise of that power is bottomed on a rule of law designed for impersonal and impartial application in all similar cases, history will surely record the result as unjust.

The rule of law is defined as follows in Professor F. A. Hayek's *Road to Serfdom:*

Nothing distinguishes more clearly conditions in a free country from those in a country under arbitrary government than the observance in the former of the great principles known as the rule of law. Stripped of all technicalities, this means that government in all its actions is bound by rules fixed and announced beforehand—rules which make it possible to foresee with fair certainty how the authority will use its coercive powers in given circumstances and to plan one's individual affairs on the basis of this knowledge.

That rule was upheld in very strong language by the Supreme Court in a United Mineworkers case a few years after the First World War.

The case was argued by one who was afterward Chief Justice of the United States, the Honorable Charles E. Hughes. I remember that in his brief he traced the law from ancient times down to the present, and very clearly distinguished, as does this noted author, between freedom and arbitrary government power and both came to the same conclusion.

Injustice is not synonymous with miscarriage of justice. No system of justice is foolproof. Reasonable men may draw erroneous conclusions from a given set of facts. Fairminded men may make legal interpretations inimical to basic liberties. So long as such men—whether they be judges, prosecutors, jurors, or United States Senators—honestly endeavor to apply a definite rule of law, they may err but they are not unjust.

At this point in my remarks, I wish to make it perfectly clear that I have the highest admiration and respect for the honesty and integrity of the six senators who served on the Select Committee to Study Censure Charges. They are all able. They would not wittingly set in motion, or condone, any action that is inherently unjust. Nevertheless, in my judgment, that is the effect of their recommendations.

I cannot agree with the junior Senator from Wisconsin that one or more of the members of the select committee were so biased as to preclude their making a fair appraisal of his case. It was manifestly impossible to find six senators who had not at one time or another expressed an opinion on the controversial junior Senator from Wisconsin.

In my judgment, the junior Senator from Wisconsin should have been allowed to make his full defense before the committee. The committee denied him that right. But since the entire subject is going to be ventilated here on the Senate floor, the junior Senator from Wisconsin will have his day in court.

Whatever the conclusion of the Senate, the junior Senator from Wisconsin will have had a full and fair hearing.

We have, then, a resolution of censure which six able and honest Senators think must be adopted to preserve the good name of the Senate, but which strikes me as patently unjust. What is the reason for these radically different conclusions?

If a court tried and punished a man without citing any law to support its action, all lawyers would condemn the result as unjust, and this would be true no matter how skillfully the proceedings were decked out in the trappings of justice. It would be no defense for the court to cite its general authority to try and punish individuals. Judicial power to punish is limited by the necessity for an applicable law, common or statutory, which defines the crime with reasonable precision.

Legislative power to punish under Article I, section 5, of the Constitution, should necessarily be exercised in accordance with the same limitations. It is even more important that in this proceeding we observe the basic tenets of Anglo-American criminal law because the exercise of our power to punish by way of censure is not judicially reviewable. The law we apply must be sought primarily in a body of legislative precedent. Occasionally, some new precedent must be formulated. But if we censure a colleague without reaffirming or establishing a precedent for all similar cases that now exist or which may exist in the future, the verdict of history will be that we were unjust.

There is no precedent for censuring a senator on the two charges set forth in the report of the select committee. The committee concedes this point on page 61 of its report. The absence of precedent, I agree, does not conclusively settle the question. If the precedent created by censure of the junior Senator from Wisconsin is to be applied impartially to all present and future senators, then censure, however unwise, would not smack of legislative tyranny. That is not the case, however. Censuring the junior Senator from Wisconsin would not establish any general precedent. It is not seriously intended to establish such a precedent. And because no such precedent would be established, we would be punishing Senator McCarthy in total disregard of any rule of law.

This issue in the case towers above all others. Yet it is not even discussed in the report of the select committee. The committee's action seems to rest on the naïve assumption that a resolution of censure is admonitory; that the object of censure is merely scolded. It is punishment. For a senator, few forms of punishment are more severe. Of course, the committee had no idea of establishing a precedent under which more than half the Senate would be liable to punishment. That is why the committee regarded as irrelevant and inadmissible the derogatory statements of other senators with reference to their colleagues. That is why the committee refused to consider what other senators have said in the heat of cross-examination.

Most opponents of censure have said that it would create an undesirable precedent. Of course, if censure is voted, and if the precedent is applied impartially to present and future senators, the result would be not merely undesirable but catastrophic. The Senate could not function as a deliberative, legislative body. The truth is that censure would not establish a precedent governing the conduct of all other senators. And when we take punitive action against one senator and refuse to apply it as a precedent to others, we depart from the restraining influence of the rule of law. We become unjust.

In my judgment, the case against the junior Senator from Wisconsin stands or falls on the answer to this question: Is the standard of conduct imposed by the resolution on the junior Senator from Wisconsin to be applied impartially to all present and future senators?

MR. JENNER. Mr. President, will the Senator from Ohio yield in order that the absence of a quorum may be suggested? I think he is making a very fine presentation of the matter. The prosecution has been heard. I think the defense should be heard. The Senate has met to consider this question, and there is no reason why all senators should not be present.

MR. BRICKER. I appreciate the offer of the Senator from Indiana, but I should like to continue so that I may complete my statement. It may be read in the *Record*. If the absence of a quorum were suggested, I doubt that more senators would remain than the number now present. So I refuse to yield for that purpose, if it does not offend the distinguished Senator from Indiana.

I have searched the rules, Mr. President, and I find no rule in the established rules of the Senate which would provide any punishment for the acts that are here charged as offenses.

Every senator must know in his heart that the answer to the following question is "No": Is the standard of conduct imposed by the resolution on the junior Senator from Wisconsin to be applied impartially to all present and future senators?

In any event, the fact can be demonstrated beyond any shadow of doubt. It is simply a job of selecting several examples from the many thousands that are available, even if they are undesired by most of us.

Turning now to the committee report, I shall not unduly extend these remarks by pointing to its many inconsistencies, or to the quality of the argument submitted. It is enough to know that censure is recommended on two of the forty-six charges presented to the committee, and that the recommendations on these two charges were influenced by two other charges discussed at length in the report. Briefly stated, the four major complaints against the junior Senator from Wisconsin are:

First. That he did not avail himself of the opportunity to appear before the Gillette subcommittee which was inquiring into matters antedating his election to the Senate, which issued no subpena to require his attendance and which denied him the right to cross-examine witnesses which, incidentally, the Watkins select committee found inexcusable;

Second. That his public statement with reference to the junior Senator from New Jersey [Mr. Hendrickson] was vulgar and insulting;

Third. That his conduct in the cross-examination of General Zwicker was inexcusable; and

Fourth. That his invitation to Federal employees to supply him with information on governmental operations "without expressly excluding therefrom classified documents, tends to create a disruption of the orderly and constitutional functioning of the executive and legislative branches." Though not made a ground for censure, the select committee added: "Such conduct cannot be condoned and is deemed improper."

I shall take up these complaints in order to show that adoption of a resolution of censure based on or influenced by them would not establish a precedent for all other members of the United States Senate.

With reference to complaint No. 1, other senators have not been, and never will be, censured for declining to accept a committee's invitation to appear, or for declining to appear voluntarily to explain conduct which took place in a prior Congress, or for refusing to cooperate with a committee not permitting them to cross-examine witnesses. Approval of this charge would not lead to censure of other senators who have in the past, and will in the future, construe an invitation as something that they have the choice of accepting or declining. Therefore, I am constrained to say that censure on the basis of this flimsy charge would reflect a vindictive passion unworthy of the world's greatest deliberative body.

In regard to complaint No. 2, what happens if we censure the junior Senator from Wisconsin for using vulgar language with reference to the junior Senator from New Jersey?—and I do not condone it. More vulgar, in my judgment, was the speech made on the Senate floor several months ago against the Senator from Wisconsin. Will the Senate censure that senator? Of course not. I do not think it should. The rules of the Senate provide that such a senator may be required to take his seat at the time when he makes such a remark on the floor of the Senate, and that thereafter he may be allowed to proceed to speak only by an affirmative vote of his colleagues; but the rule makes no reference regarding censure for what was said. But if only the junior Senator from Wisconsin is to be censured for using intemperate language reflecting adversely on other senators, how is the Senate to defend itself against charges of being unjust and discriminatory? If uncomplimentary references by one senator concerning another will put the censure machinery in motion, there will be no time here for anything except mutual recrimination. Nothing of the sort will happen, as we know. That being true, how can censure of the junior Senator from Wisconsin be based on anything except an avidity to punish?

Censure on the basis of complaint No. 3 would establish no precedent applicable to the conduct of other senators. Whatever the outcome of this proceeding, in examining uncooperative witnesses senators will continue to follow the example and advice furnished by Mr. Justice Black on the value of vigorous cross-examination.

I believe that General Zwicker—and I may say I have read all the testimony—was an irritating, evasive, and arrogant witness. If I should say now, and without the excuse of provocation, that General Zwicker is not fit to wear the uniform of his country, would I be censured; or would any other member of the Senate be censured for saying such a thing? Will a member of the so-called crime-investigating committee be censured for showing less respect for the rights of witnesses appearing before the special crime committee than the junior Senator from Wisconsin shows to witnesses appearing before his committee? Certainly not. And I would oppose any such move.

If the Senator's public criticism of General Zwicker is an adequate basis for censure, will the Senator who has charged General Zwicker's boss, the Secretary of Defense, with favoritism or corruption, or both, in awarding defense contracts and, therefore, necessarily unfit to be a Cabinet officer, be the next one to be subjected to a demand that he be censured? No, Mr. President, the Senate will not censure him, and all of us know it. Just think how many senators could be censured for charging that the Secretary of the Interior, notwithstanding his constitutional oath, has been giving away property of the United States with the profligacy of a spendthrift internationalist. However, none of these possible censure actions will ever materialize, even if the junior Senator from Wisconsin is censured. Precisely because the censure of the junior Senator from Wisconsin will not create a precedent of general applicability, we would deny him the impersonal justice which from time immemorial has been symbolized by a blindfold on the figure of justice.

To whatever extent complaint No. 4 influenced the action of the Select Committee to Study Censure, the senior Senator from Utah [Mr. Watkins] and his colleagues on the Senate Internal Security Subcommittee would be likely candidates for censure. They signed a report inviting Federal employees to furnish the committee information relative to subversion, and, in the words of the report of the select committee, "without expressly excluding therefrom classified documents." Of course, they will not be censured, whatever the fate of the junior Senator from Wisconsin, and they should not be. They were within their rights, under the law. It must be a strong, holier-than-thou obsession which prevents a senator from seeing the unparalleled absurdity of the situation in which the Senate now finds itself.

I wish now to qualify slightly my previous statements that a vote of censure will not constitute a precedent. It may establish a very narrow precedent, but nevertheless an exceedingly dangerous one. The precedent would operate as a club to beat down any senator inclined to lead in Congress the never-ending fight—and I hope it is never ending—against the Communist conspiracy in America.

It is not mere coincidence that the main stream of vilification and abuse has been directed toward those members of Congress who have been active on the committees which expose Communists and their retinue of dupes and fellow travelers. From the time of Martin Dies, in the thirties, the strategy of the Communist conspiracy has been to defame and destroy those men in Congress who symbolize the opposition of millions of patriotic Americans. The Communist strategy has been sound: Destroy the symbol first, and then the forces represented and made articulate by the symbol can be much more easily crushed. The Communist strategy has been exceedingly well executed.

Now a word about methods in this life-or-death struggle with the Communist conspiracy. All of us have seen the grisly face of communism. Not all of us have reacted in the same way. Though all of us have gazed on the same evil countenance, our interpretations of the vision have not been uniform.

To the junior Senator from Wisconsin and to me, the gory mien of communism appears as unmitigated evil. The reaction of the junior Senator from Wisconsin has been simple and direct. With patriotic exuberance, he grabbed his shillelagh and went to work. Some of his friendly critics suggest that he should use a rapier, and other friendly critics tell him that a strong spotlight is sufficient.

There is another class of senators in whom the frightful face of communism arouses no strong emotion. They pretend that the evil vision is some optical illusion. These critics of McCarthyism urge that communism be discussed in broad and general terms; that the prime necessity of the hour is preservation of an expansive power; and that the only gentlemanly way to fight Communists is with both hands tied behind the back.

Most of the fanatical critics of McCarthyism are technically non-Communists. But the brutal face of communism holds them in the irresistible power of sensual attraction. Logically they know that to embrace communism is fatal. Yet they cannot tolerate any congressional attack on this perfected evil. And why not? Because the vision of communism is so strikingly similar to socialism and other collectivisms to which they have pledged their lives, their fortunes, and whatever small honor may exist in such a cause.

That, in a nutshell, is the meaning of the debate over McCarthy's methods. The primary function of congressional investigation in this field is to inform and to alert the American people concerning all aspects of the Communist conspiracy, and to lay the foundation for legislation. In fulfilling that function the junior Senator from Wisconsin has been preeminently successful. He has dramatized the issue better than anyone else. Deservedly or not, his friends and enemies, both here and abroad, have made him the prime symbol of vigorous anticommunism. The question here and now is whether we shall destroy that symbol in a spirit of vengeance or whether we shall preserve it in the tradition of equal justice under the law.

Today the hue and cry is on throughout the land. The pack which hunts the hunters of Communists has caught the smell of blood. Without any implication of bad faith or lack of patriotism on the part of any of my colleagues, whom I respect, I shall not run with that pack.

EDUCATION

THE COMMON GROUND OF HUMILITY [1]

J. BARTLET BREBNER [2]

Dr. John Bartlet Brebner, Gouverneur Morris Professor of History at Columbia, the University Orator, gave this address at the Charter Day Convocation of Columbia University held in the Cathedral of St. John the Divine, October 31, 1954. The audience of eight thousand included Queen Mother Elizabeth of England, West German Chancellor Konrad Adenauer, the Vice President of India, the Secretary General of the United Nations, Chief Justice Earl Warren of the United States Supreme Court, and Adlai E. Stevenson, as well as many scholars and other statesmen from both hemispheres. The cathedral ceremony ended a full year's celebration in honor of the founding of the university (on October 31, 1754, King George II signed the charter of King's College, later Columbia University). The Queen Mother and forty-seven other distinguished visitors received honorary degrees.

Dr. Brebner had interrupted his term as visiting professor at St. John's College, Cambridge University, to return to New York for the closing ceremonies of the bicentennial.

This discourse analyzed with unusual insight the scholars' present dilemmas. A major solution was found in humility as the common ground of the academic and non-academic groups: "Humility is man's best common ground." This eloquent plea for scholarly humility was singularly appropriate for the distinguished audience, representing as it did the intellectual leadership, national and international, of the day. Original, too, was the speaker's oral style, authentic in its rhythm, selective and suggestive in its phrasing—eloquently expressed in its perspicuity, its propriety, and its figurative associations.

Mr. President, members of the university and distinguished guests:

We are gathered today for the advancement of scholarship. We all find reassurance in our common aim to practice and to cherish it. It is fitting, for example, that our royal guest is

[1] The text is from the New York *Times*, November 1, 1954, as approved by Dr. Brebner, through whose courtesy this reprint appears.

[2] For biographical note, see Appendix.

a scholar—a barrister-at-law, a Master of the Bench of the Middle Temple and once its treasurer. When, as the Court Circular puts it, she "is pleased to dine in Hall tonight," her fellow-benchers are also pleased, for they enjoy her learning, her alert mind and her charm.

Today, as two hundred years ago, scholars and the friends of scholars are alarmed by the world they live in and by the threats that it utters against the life of the sensibilities and of the mind.   Today, therefore, it seems worth recalling how, only five years after our university was founded, two great Europeans gave vent to their melancholy about a world that was then submerged in the horrors of the Seven Years' War. Voltaire's hero, Candide, having miraculously survived pandemonium, finally cut short his tutor's incurable optimism by reminding him that they must cultivate their garden. Dr. Johnson's hero, Rasselas, having viewed the miseries of the world, which his tutor had told him could alone serve as measuring-rods for his blissful but boring existence in Abyssinia, abandoned his hopes for perfect happiness, and decided to go back home as soon as the Nile's inundation should retreat.

It has been said that Voltaire's melancholy was of the mind, whereas Dr. Johnson's was of the heart. Whatever the case, it was in *Rasselas* that Johnson made a memorable pronouncement about "the life, that is devoted to knowledge."   He said:

> To talk in public, to think in solitude, to read and hear, to inquire, and answer inquiries, is the business of a scholar. He wanders about the world without pomp or terror, and is neither known nor valued but by men like himself.

Probably Columbia's first president, also Samuel Johnson, would have agreed completely with his namesake.   Equally probably, while most of us here would agree as to "the business of a scholar," yet we would question the description of how he gets along with his world.   What is it that seems to have been happening since 1759 to prevent scholars from wandering about the world without pomp or terror, and from being neither known nor valued but by men like themselves?

Many of the very large changes during the past two centuries will immediately come to mind: the great social processes of literacy and of communications that interact so as to disseminate knowledge and doctrine world-wide almost instantaneously; the great economic processes of mechanized production and of rapid transportation that have made the world's peoples live for the most part very artificially in cities; the great political processes of democracy and socialism that have put power over men and goods in the hands of mere majorities; and the great intellectual processes whereby crudely determined utilitarianism or materialism often eclipses broader and deeper considerations that men have derived from tradition, from religion and from the arts. But how have these processes affected the scholar?

Chiefly they appear to have been narrowing for all men, including scholars, the bases and freedom for judgment. Every moment new reading, hearing or seeing blurs the past, exalts the present and sets out will-o'-the-wisps in the future. Industrialization, rapid transportation and urbanization seem constantly to secrete poisons that almost counterbalance their potentialities for well-being. Some democracies have demonstrated the ease of surrender to tyrants, and some socialistic institutions have proved to be almost necessarily authoritarian. And, finally, considerations of utility or practicality contain a strong bias towards the short run, and thereby tend to stifle deeper and perhaps surer thought directed towards more abidingly fruitful ends.

These processes have been obvious and these fears have become commonplaces. Yet are not such simplicities, such absolutes, nearly always misleading? Has man ever submitted to absolutes? Has he not normally lived in ambiguity? Has he not depended upon uneasy compromises among forces that his best thinkers have been able to delineate, but that his best men of action have never been able to master? And, if this is so, what seems to be the principal ambiguity in which we find ourselves today?

It is, of course, the most ancient and comprehensive human dilemma that we know, that between pride and humility, a dilemma if we regard these as equal evils, an ambiguity if we think that each may be a mixture of evil and good. Superficially our circumstances appear to favor pride, to encourage the growth of that arrogance, that *hubris,* which the ancient wisdoms of Asia and Europe portrayed as the sure road to destruction. Our knowledge of nuclear fission and fusion, for instance, might serve as a symbol of power whose use depends on human vacillations between pride and humility. The same thing might be said about the use of mass communications, or the production and distribution of goods, or the organization and exercise of political power. In fact, it is the agglomeration of physical power, social power, economic power and propagandistic power, as the potentially single prize for which artists in political power contend, that most alarms the community of scholars. For politics is an art of the immediate, and statesmanship, which rests on longer, deeper views, is rare.

Yet there may be a counterbalance in the other half of our embracing ambiguity, that is to say, in humility. A century ago, when Tennyson was wrestling with his form of our problem, he burst out:

> There lives more faith in honest doubt,
> Believe me, than in half the creeds.

Indeed, when one thinks of how man has, for thousands of years, somehow barely escaped destruction from the evil in his nature, it is tempting to believe that his margin of survival has been provided by his humility, by his recognition of the limits to his powers and to his wisdom in using them.

Be that as it may, it seems worth suggesting to an academic audience that in humility they may find common ground with other men that will provide a surer footing than will pride. Emerson once complained that "we cannot be willing to say I do not know." And yet, since his time, a common saying has struck root in the United States, the phrase "I could be wrong." Let us consider soberly the desirability of trying to make it a still commoner saying.

During recent years, a hurricane of investigations and persecutions has lashed those parts of the earth where men in political authority have conceived themselves to be compelled to maintain one set of values and to attack all others. Throughout these operations, nothing has been more dreadful than the common assumption that every man must at all times be "right."

Surely this intolerance of variation is *hubris*—the insolent vain-glory and self-assurance that the Greeks denominated the basic, the suicidal, sin. In our time this sin may take the form of worshiping the power over nature or over human nature, or the deification of a man, an economic entity, a political party or a nation state.

We academic persons know better than this—indeed true scholars are by nature humble—but many of us forget that non-academic persons know better, too. Each group, they and we, is largely to blame for being misunderstood, and therefore for being mistrusted, by the other. Let us then, for our part, exalt and extend our knowledge by all means, but let us also constantly assert our uncertainties, our ambiguities, and there-fore our eternal need to know and to think more. If we do so, it seems likely that non-academic persons will be quick to rec-ognize that we and they are similar individuals, in the same boat on perilous waters, and that they will the more trustingly pool their skills with ours in guiding its voyage.

Scholarship, that is to say, the most perfected form of knowl-edge, is non-academic as well as academic. Both kinds of true scholarship are humble and inquiring. Humility is man's best common ground. If that ground is properly surveyed and delin-eated, it seems reasonable to believe that there will be fewer attempts to impose limits on man's right to knowledge and its use.

And, finally, through humility we might expect to regain the salutary sense of the absurdity of man, laugh a little more at ourselves, and be better prepared for being laughed at. If we could thus offset our sense of doom, and restore the balance of the comic and the tragic that is man's fate, it is at least con-ceivable that our poets, our prophets and our other artists might flourish in communion with a broader and a more ap-preciative public than they have recently been able to enlist.

COMMENCEMENT ADDRESS [3]

EDWARD R. MURROW [4]

Edward R. Murrow gave this commencement address at Hamilton College, Clinton, New York, on June 6, 1954, before two thousand persons in the Sage Hockey Building. Others heard it outdoors over a loudspeaker.

At the conclusion Mr. Murrow was given an honorary degree, Doctor of Humane Letters, with the following citation:

As citizens in a democracy we can act no better than we know. Much of what we know must come to us from those who have a passion for getting facts and to that end, a willingness to forgo the blandishments of the armchair and the easy life. You are such a person. A Carolinian by birth, a graduate of Washington State College, you were with the Columbia Broadcasting System developing educational programs in Europe when your coverage of the Austrian *anschluss* developed a new profession: foreign correspondent for radio. You have since been the eyes and the ears of millions, bringing to them objectively, unswervingly, facts as you find them, be they in the suite of a prime minister, in a plane on a bombing raid, or in a trench under fire. You have put great faith in the intelligence of the American public—and rightly so. But more, you have imbued others with your passion for facts, for truth, and for adult presentation over radio and television until the level of your whole profession has been raised and the people of your country by that much better prepared for citizenship in a democracy.

Identified with the Columbia Broadcasting system since 1935, Mr. Murrow was from 1945 to 1947 vice president in charge of news and educational programs. In 1955 he is still continuing his daily radio broadcasts. In addition, since 1951 he has produced *See It Now,* a weekly television program, and more recently he has added another television show, *Person to Person.*

In contrast with other TV-radio commentators he is not primarily an orator-persuader. He does not preach (except as he closes his daily broadcasts with apt quotations). Although his opinions sometimes show forth, his statements are couched in restrained language that probably

[3] Text furnished through the courtesy of Herbert Hansen, assistant to President Robert W. McEwen, of Hamilton College. The address was delivered extemporaneously, tape recorded, and transcribed. Reprinted here through the courtesy of Mr. Murrow and the Columbia Broadcasting Company.

[4] For biographical note, see Appendix.

conciliates many opponents. His appeal is mainly through clear exposition.

Mr. Murrow has an unusually good radio voice. He is conversational, free from vocal passion. His voice transmits an agreeable personality.[5]

Mr. President, sir, gentlemen of Hamilton, and especially the class of 1954: You have done me considerable honor in inviting me here today, and I think it was Shakespeare who said "Beggar that I am, I am even poor in thanks."

I would deny at the outset the title—orator. But you will appreciate that this is a rather difficult assignment for one who is accustomed to working with microphones and cameras, because they both be marvelously neutral. There is no case upon the record of a camera or a microphone falling asleep, indicating boredom or walking out in the middle of a paragraph. I cannot promise you clarity on any subject but I shall be brief, for brevity is good both when we are and are not understood. . . .

One of the most significant facts that I have discovered in the course of my limited research on this institution, is the fact that it was founded upon bed rock. I have, in the course of my travels, encountered a considerable number of graduates of this institution. They have always, it seemed to me, had a tendency to stand steady in their shoes, a remarkable degree of intellectual independence, and not always a noticeable tendency to conform. I should like to examine briefly some aspects of the bed rock of this confused civilization, which you young gentlemen, I trust, are soon going to make efforts to change. I would suggest that throughout our national history we have generally sought and found easy and quick solutions, with one exception. We now find ourselves thrust into a position of world leadership where there are no easy or quick solutions, and where indeed there may be no solutions at all. This will require more patience, more fortitude, more understanding on your part than has been required of previous university generations.

You will recognize, I am sure, that we are regarded abroad with a mixture of fear and admiration, and that in some areas

[5] For further comment on Mr. Murrow, see the Index of this volume, for his earlier speeches.

the fear outweighs the admiration. You will, I am sure, agree that this world leadership has been thrust upon us, but we have no alternative. Because unless the freedom of the individual, the dignity of the individual, the due process of law, survive on this continent, it will survive nowhere on this earth.

We were chatting this morning a little about security—how it is to be achieved. I do not know the answer, but I will make you a suggestion as to how you might achieve a degree of security. I have seen other people achieve it.

Don't write anything, don't talk about basic issues, don't associate, don't believe that you have any responsibility, except to do what you can to make sure that no one subsequently will say to you—"you were wrong," confuse dissent with disloyalty, confuse accusation with conviction—through these methods it would be possible, I suppose, to secure a degree of temporary, personal security at the cost of creating an intellectual and moral desert—which in due course would be taken over by designing men, who are to be found in all countries, at all periods.

The right to be wrong is quite as important as the right to be admired, and I trust you will exercise it.

It seems to me that for generations each graduating class has been told that you are going out from the cloistered academic life and into a world beset with doubt, uncertainty and fear. I am quite aware that it is an error to give good advice and it is almost fatal to attempt advice at all. But it has always seemed to me that commencement speakers—one, should be more brief than they are, and the other, that they should be more practical in the counsel they give. It really doesn't matter because no graduating class has ever been influenced or guided by its commencement speaker. So here I offer you a few concrete bits of advice. . . . For those graduates inclined to be argumentative, a word from William Hazlitt: "We are not satisfied to be right, unless we can prove others to be quite wrong."

To the graduate who barely squeaked by in Latin—this from the German poet Heinrich Heine: "Had the Romans been obliged to learn Latin, they never would have had time to conquer the world." . . .

To the holder of the sheepskin whose manners have not been polished as well as they might have been: "Be kind and considerate to others, depending somewhat upon whom they are." . . .

Advice for the student who wants to be a writer, from Don Marquis: "If you want to get rich from writing, write the kind of things where people move their lips when they read it." . . .

All of these words of wisdom will of course be forgotten just like all commencement speeches. So let's return to the traditional theme. This year's graduates are being told to have courage. Channing Pollock once said that "No man on earth has more courage than the man who can stop after eating one peanut."

I have an idea that a wholly serious commencement address could be done in a single paragraph and it would go something like this:

Graduates who have achieved this distinction by hard work, cheating or the indifference of your professors, you have had a good break. Not one of you paid your own freight. No matter how wealthy your parents, how exclusive your school, society in general has paid part of the cost of your superior intellectual training, and you are in the debt of that society. That sheepskin won't get or hold a job for you. It doesn't guarantee you personal profit at the expense of the society which made possible your superior training. Somewhere along the way you must have picked up some ideas about the dignity and the freedom of the individual, about his right to be wrong, and his rights under the law. You have finished your education in a time of uncertainty, unrest and unprecedented change. Don't overdevelop your instinct for being unhappy. Don't conclude prematurely that the individual is unimportant and that he can abdicate his responsibility for making the tough, hard decisions that you may wrestle with for most of your lives. You are of the at least partially educated brood of the most powerful nation on earth. You live in a country that is fat while much of the world is either lean or hungry. There will be all kinds of alarums and excursions and times when you will want to say "Let someone else make these hard decisions as to what our policy and our purpose should be."

These words were written by the great German poet and philosopher—Goethe. Just for the beauty of the language and the clarity of the thought, I should like to read my single-paragraph commencement address. He said there are nine requisites for contented living: Health enough to make work a pleasure; wealth enough to support your needs; strength enough to battle with your difficulties and overcome them; grace enough to confess your sins and forsake them; patience enough to toil until some good is accomplished; charity enough to see some good in your neighbor; love enough to move you to be useful and helpful to others; faith enough to make real the things of God; hope enough to remove all anxious fear concerning the future.

And, gentlemen, I would that I could have bared for you the bed rock of this disordered world. You have to do your own digging for truth. But beware of those who tell you where to dig, or what implements you should use. Whether you like it or not you are going to make a small scratch on the bed rock of history. I have seen certain Americans, Britons, Frenchmen in South Korea, who have died in order that you might have the opportunity to make that mark—the opportunity in a real sense to be a pivot upon which history turns. Whole nations have lived and died without having the opportunity that we have to be decisive upon the history of our time when it comes to be written. Physical courage is a commodity in plentiful supply. It is not always easy to stand steady in defense of those intangible principles. You are free men today not because of accident but because other men were willing to pay the price of defending our freedom both domestically and in the foreign field. Freedom is not something that is to be had in a bargain basement. It is not something that can be paid for in a lump sum. It must be bought on the installment plan and each generation must pay a part of the price.

Unless the principles embedded in our basic document survive here in this country, they will, in all truth, survive nowhere. I envy you. I doubt that any of you would choose to live in more tranquil times. I hope not.

I would end this dreary, and I hope not too long discourse, by saying one final word, which I take from J. M. Barrie who once made a commencement address at St. Andrew's in the years immediately following the end of the First World War. And he ended it by saying, "Gentlemen, face the unknown with a cheer."

EDUCATIONAL DEFICIT AND
NATIONAL CRISIS [6]

WALTER LIPPMANN [7]

Walter Lippmann gave this address on March 19, 1954, at a dinner of the National Citizens Commission for the Public Schools, then meeting in its fifth annual assembly, at the Fairmont Hotel, in San Francisco.

This Commission was organized in 1949 to help deal with the problem of the nation-wide shortage of school facilities, and to "arouse in each community the intelligence and will to improve our public schools."

The speech itself was developed in Mr. Lippmann's usual historical-philosophical vein. The speaker set forth the problem of this "age of disorder and upheaval, the decline of the West," by contrasting the state of political affairs in 1900 with those of 1954.

A philosopher, he traced the decline of democracy to our failures in properly educating our citizenry. He even resorted to statistics to illustrate the decline in our educational efforts, as shown by our spendings for education as compared with our total Federal expenditures.

His appeal for an educational "will" was brief and doubtless needed expansion to stimulate decisive and immediate action.

This address should be read in the light of Mr. Lippmann's forty years of theorizing about man and education. His speeches have been largely analytical, philosophical, rather than concretely constructive and action-bearing.

At Harvard and afterward he was largely influenced by such philosophers as William James, Isaiah Royce, George Santayana, and Graham Wallas. This speech, like his others, is characterized by sanity, aloofness, and only moderate emotionalism. This speaker-writer, avoiding exuberance, is always clear and methodical in unfolding his thesis.

Walter Lippmann's writings, books and thrice-weekly columns in some 182 syndicated newspapers, have doubtless had an important influence on American thought. In 1953, 111 American editors and editorial writers, rating columnists on the basis of their reliability, fairness, and skill in analyzing the news, placed him at the top.

On occasion Mr. Lippmann speaks without notes. In talking over the radio or on formal occasions, he writes his address and follows it closely. He once stated, "I do not think of myself as a public speaker."

[6] By permission of and through the courtesy of Mr. Walter Lippmann. The text was furnished by the National Citizens Commission for the Public Schools.

[7] For biographical note, see Appendix.

Nevertheless, he has a well-modulated, pleasing voice, which expresses his intelligence and cultural training. He avoids oratory or many gestures, but he is alive, responsive to his ideas, and creates effective audience rapport.[8]

It is a privilege and an honor to be a speaker in this gathering, and for me it is also a special personal pleasure to come back to this city. I like San Francisco very much—so much that I am always glad of a reason for coming here. And so I accepted Mr. Larsen's generous invitation to speak this evening, long before I realized—from the trouble of preparing my speech —that I would be making a short speech on a very big subject.

I should tell you at once that I have not been a diligent and useful member of the National Citizens Commission for the Public Schools. My record of attendance at its meetings is deplorable. I have done virtually no homework. I can claim no good marks for effort, much less for any contribution of my own to the important work of the Commission.

Yet, for this particular occasion, when I shall be saying things that some of you may think controversial, my bad record has one compensating advantage. Nothing that I shall say can be charged against Mr. Larsen and my fellow commissioners. They have not seen me often enough, or at close enough range, to have rubbed off upon me—if I may paraphrase a current heresy—any responsibility by association.

What I am going to say is the result of a prolonged exposure to the continuing crisis of our Western society—to the crisis of the democratic governments and of free institutions during the wars and revolutions of the twentieth century. Now it does not come easily to anyone who—like me—has breathed the soft air of the world before the wars that began in 1914—who has known a world that was not divided and frightened and full of hate—it does not come easily to such a man to see clearly and to measure coolly the times we live in. The scale and scope and the complexity of our needs is without any precedent in our experience, and indeed—we may fairly say—in all human experience.

[8] For further comment on Mr. Lippmann as a speaker, see *Representative American Speeches: 1940-41*, p292-309.

In 1900 men everywhere on earth acknowledged, even when they resented, the leadership of the Western nations. It was taken for granted that the liberal democracies were showing the way towards the good life in the good society, and few had any doubts of the eventual, but certain, progress of all mankind towards more democracy and a wider freedom.

The only question was when—the question was never whether—the less fortunate and the more backward peoples of the world would have learned to use not only the technology of the West but also the political institutions of the West. All would soon be learning to decide the issues which divided them by free and open and rational discussion; they would soon learn how to conduct free and honest elections, to administer justice. Mankind would come to accept and comprehend the idea that all men are equally under the laws and all men must have the equal protection of the laws.

At the beginning of this century the acknowledged model of a new government, even in Russia, was a liberal democracy in the British or the French or the American style. Think what has happened to the Western world and to its ideas and ideals during the forty years since the world wars began. The hopes that men then took for granted are no longer taken for granted. The institutions and the way of life which we have inherited, and which we cherish, have lost their paramount, their almost undisputed, hold upon the allegiance and the affections and the hopes of the peoples of the earth. They are no longer universally accepted as being the right way towards the good life on this earth. They are fiercely challenged abroad. They are widely doubted and they are dangerously violated even here at home.

During this half-century the power of the Western democratic nations has been declining. Their influence upon the destiny of the great masses of mankind has been shrinking. We are the heirs of the proudest tradition of government in the history of mankind. Yet we no longer find ourselves talking now—as we did before the First World War—about the progress of liberal democracy among the awakening multitudes of mankind. We are talking now about the defense and the survival of liberal democracy in its contracted area.

We are living in an age of disorder and upheaval. Though the United States has grown powerful and rich, we know in our hearts that we have become, at the same time, insecure and anxious. Our people enjoy an abundance of material things, such as no large community of men have ever known. But our people are not happy about their position or confident about their future. For we are not sure whether our responsibilities are not greater than our power and our wisdom.

We have been raised to the first place in the leadership of the Western society at a time when the general civilization of the West has suffered a spectacular decline and is gravely threatened. We, who have become so suddenly the protecting and the leading power of that civilization, are not clear and united among ourselves about where we are going and how we should deal with our unforeseen responsibilities, our unwanted mission, our unexpected duties.

It is an awe-inspiring burden that we find ourselves compelled to bear. We have suddenly acquired responsibilities for which we were not prepared—for which we are not now prepared—for which, I am very much afraid, we are not now preparing ourselves.

We have had, and probably we must expect for a long time to have, dangerous and implacable enemies. But if we are to revive and recover, and are to go forward again, we must not look for the root of the trouble in our adversaries. We must look for it in ourselves. We must rid ourselves of the poison of self-pity. We must have done with the falsehood that all would be well were it not that we are the victims of wicked and designing men.

In 1914, when the decline of the West began, no one had heard of Lenin, Trotsky, Mussolini, Hitler, Stalin, and Mao Tse-tung. We have not fallen from our preeminence because we have been attacked. It would be much truer to say, and it is nobler to say it, that we have been attacked because our capacity to cope with our tasks had begun to decline.

We shall never have the spirit to revive and to recover so long as we try to console ourselves by shutting our eyes, and by wringing our hands and beating our breasts and filling the air with complaints that we have been weakened because we were attacked, and that we have been making mistakes because we were betrayed.

We must take the manly view, which is that the failure of the Western democracies during this catastrophic half of the twentieth century is due to the failings of the democratic peoples. They have been attacked and brought down from their preeminence because they have lacked the clarity of purpose and the resolution of mind and of heart to cope with the accumulating disasters and disorders. They have lacked the clarity of purpose and the resolution of mind and of heart to prevent the wars that have ruined the West, to prepare for these wars they could not prevent, and, having won them at last after exorbitant sacrifice and at a ruinous cost, to settle those wars and to restore law and order upon the face of the globe.

I have said all this because it is only in the context of our era that we can truly conceive the problem of educating the American democracy. When we do that, we must, I believe, come to see that the effort we are making to educate ourselves as a people is not nearly equal to our needs and to our responsibilities.

If we compare our total effort—in public and private schools, and from kindergarten through college—with what it was fifty years ago, the quantitative increase is impressive. We are offering much more schooling of a more expensive kind to very many more pupils. By every statistical measure, the United States has made striking quantitative progress during the past century towards the democratic goal of universal education. The typical young American is spending more years in school than his father or grandfather; a much higher proportion of young people are going to high school and beyond; and more dollars—even discounting the depreciation of the dollar—are being spent for each person's education.

Now, if it were no more difficult to live in the United States today than it was fifty years ago, that is to say if life were as simple as it was then—if the problems of private and community life were as easily understood—if the task of governing the United States at home, and of conducting its foreign relations abroad, were as uncomplicated and no more dangerous than it was fifty years ago—then we could celebrate, we could be happy, we could be congratulating ourselves that we are making great progress in the task of educating ourselves as a democracy.

But we cannot make that comforting comparison without deceiving ourselves seriously. We cannot measure the demands upon our people in the second half of the twentieth century,— the demands in terms of trained intelligence, moral discipline, knowledge, and, not least, the wisdom of great affairs—by what was demanded of them at the beginning of the first half of this century. The burden of living in America today and of governing America today is very much heavier than it was fifty years ago, and the crucial question is whether the increase of our effort in education is keeping up with the increase in the burden.

When we use this standard of comparison, we must find, I submit, that the increase in our effort to educate ourselves is of a quite different—and of a very much smaller—order of magnitude than is the increase in what is demanded of us in this divided and dangerous world. Our educational effort and our educational needs are not now anywhere nearly in balance. The supply is not nearly keeping up with the demand. The burden of the task is very much heavier than is the strength of the effort. There is a very serious and dangerous deficit between the output of education and our private and public need to be educated.

How can we measure this discrepancy? I am sorry to say that I shall have to use a few figures, trusting that none of you will think that when I use them, I am implying that all things can be measured in dollars and cents. I am using the figures because there is no other way to illustrate concretely the difference in the two orders of magnitude—the difference between what we do to educate ourselves, on the one hand, and on the other hand, what the kind of world we live in demands of us.

What shall we use as a measure of our educational effort? For the purpose of the comparison, I think we may take the total expenditure per capita, first in 1900, and then about half a century later, in 1953, on public and private schools from kindergarten through college.

And as a measure of the burden of our task—of the responsibilities and of the commitments to which education has
now to be addressed—we might take Federal expenditures per
capita, first in 1900, and then in our time, half a century later.

We differ among ourselves, of course, as to whether we are
spending too much, too little, or the right amount, on defense,
and on the public services. But these differences do not seriously
affect the argument. For all of us—or nearly all of us—are
agreed on the general size and the scope of the necessary tasks
of the modern Federal Government, both in military defense
and for civilian purposes. Between the highest and the lowest
proposals of responsible and informed men, I doubt that the
difference is as much as 20 per cent. That is not a great enough
difference to affect the point I am making. That point is that
the size of the public expenditure reflects—roughly, of course,
but nevertheless, fundamentally—the scale and scope of what
we are impelled and compelled to do. It registers our judgment
on the problems which we must cope with.

Now, in 1900, the educational effort—measured in expenditures per capita—was $3.40. The task—as measured by Federal
expenditure per capita—was $6.85. What we must be interested
in is, I submit, the ratio between these two figures. We find,
then, that in 1900 the nation put out $1 of educational effort
against $2 of public task.

How is it now, half a century or so later? In 1953, the
educational effort was at the rate of about $76 per capita. Federal
expenditures—including defense—had risen to $467 per capita.
The ratio of educational effort to public task, which in 1900 was
as one is to two, had fallen a half century later, to a ratio of one
to six.

Perhaps I should pause at this point for a parenthesis to
say for those, who may be thinking how much the value of the
dollar has depreciated since 1900, that I am aware of that, but
for the purposes of this comparison, it makes no difference. For
while the dollar was worth probably three times as much in 1900
as in 1953, we are interested only in the relative effort in 1900
and in 1953. The ratio would be the same if we divided the

1953 expenditures by three, or if we multiplied the 1900 expenditures by three.

You have now heard all the statistics that I shall use. The two ratios, the one at the beginning of our rise to the position of the leading great power of the world and the other the ratio a half century later, when we carry the enormous burden abroad and at home—these two ratios show, I submit, that the effort we are now making to educate ourselves has fallen in relation to our needs.

I must now remind you that this disparity between the educational effort and the public task is in fact greater than the figures suggest. For in this half century there has been a momentous change in the structure of American society, and it has added greatly to the burden upon the schools.

The responsibility of the schools for educating the new generation has become very much more comprehensive than it used to be. Ever so much more is now demanded of the schools. For they are expected to perform many of the educational functions which used to be performed by the family, the settled community, the church, the family business, the family farm, the family trade.

This is a very big subject in itself—much too big for me tonight—except to mention it as a reminder that the comparison between our real educational effort and our real public need is less favorable than the figures of one as to two in 1900, as against one as to six today. For the school today has a much larger role to play in the whole process of education than it needed to play in the older American society.

Can it be denied that the educational effort is inadequate? I think it cannot be denied. I do not mean that we are doing a little too little. I mean that we are going much too little. We are entering upon an era which will test to the utmost the capacity of our democracy to cope with the gravest problems of modern times—and on a scale never yet attempted in all the history of the world. We are entering upon this difficult and dangerous period with what I believe we must call a growing deficit in the quantity and the quality of American education.

There is, I believe, compelling proof that we are operating at an educational deficit. It is to be found in many of the controversies within the educational system. I am not myself, of course, a professional educator. But I do some reading about education, and I have been especially interested in the problem of providing education for the men and women who must perform the highest functions in our society—the elucidation and the articulation of its ideals, the advancement of knowledge, the making of high policy in the government, and the leadership of the people.

How are we discussing this problem? Are we, as we ought to be doing, studying what are the subjects and what are the disciplines which are needed for the education of the gifted children for the leadership of the nation? That is not the main thing we are discussing. We are discussing whether we can afford to educate our leaders when we have so far to go before we have done what we should do to provide equal opportunities for all people.

Most of the argument—indeed the whole issue—of whether to address the effort in education to the average of ability or to the higher capacities—derives from the assumption that we have to make that choice. But why do we have to choose? Why are we not planning to educate everybody as much as everybody can be educated, some much more and some less than others?

This alleged choice is forced upon us only because our whole educational effort is too small. If we were not operating at a deficit level, our working ideal would be the fullest opportunity for all—each child according to its capacity. It is the deficit in our educational effort which compels us to deny to the children fitted for the leadership of the nation the opportunity to become educated for that task.

So we have come to the point, I would contend, where we must lift ourselves as promptly as we can to a new and much higher level of interest, of attention, of hard work, of care, of concern, of expenditure, and of dedication to the education of the American people.

We have to do in the educational system something very like what we have done in the military establishment during the past fifteen years. We have to make a break-through to a radically higher and broader conception of what is needed and of what can be done. Our educational effort today, what we think we can afford, what we think we can do, how we feel entitled to treat our schools and our teachers—all of that—is still in approximately the same position as was the military effort of this country before Pearl Harbor.

In 1940 our armed forces were still at a level designed for a policy of isolation in this hemisphere and of neutrality in any war across the two oceans. Today, the military establishment has been raised to a different and higher plateau, and the effort that goes into it is enormously greater than it was in 1940.

Our educational effort, on the other hand, has not yet been raised to the plateau of the age we live in. I am not saying, of course, that we should spend $40 billion on education because we spend about that much on defense. I am saying that we must make the same order of radical change in our attitude toward education as we have made in our attitude towards defense. We must measure our educational effort as we do our military effort. That is to say, we must measure it not by what it would be easy and convenient to do, but by what it is necessary to do in order that the nation may survive and flourish. We have learned that we are quite rich enough to defend ourselves, whatever the cost. We must now learn that we are quite rich enough to educate ourselves as we need to be educated.

There is an enormous margin of luxury in this country against which we can draw for our vital needs. We take that for granted when we think of the national defense. From the tragedies and the bitter experience of being involved in wars for which we were inadequately prepared, we have acquired the will to defend ourselves. And, having done that, having acquired the will, we have found the way. We know how to find the dollars that are needed to defend ourselves, even if we are to do without something else that is less vitally important.

In education we have not yet acquired that kind of will. But we need to acquire it, and we have no time to lose. We must acquire it in this decade. For if, in the crucial years which are coming, our people remain as unprepared as they are for their responsibilities and their mission, they may not be equal to the challenge, and if they do not succeed, they may never have a second chance in order to try again.

RELIGION

WE INTEND TO STAY TOGETHER [1]

G. Bromley Oxnam [2]

The Reverend G. Bromley Oxnam, one of the five retiring presidents of the World Council of Churches, and Bishop of the Methodist Church of the Washington, D.C. area, preached this sermon at the opening service of the Second Assembly of the World Council, in Evanston, Illinois, on Sunday morning, August 15, 1954.

The service was held in the First Methodist Church, with a seating capacity of fifteen hundred. Loudspeakers in two assembly halls and a chapel communicated the service to the large overflow audience. In the processional marched seven hundred priests and patriarchs, bishops and archbishops, ministers and laymen. The order of service with hymns and litany was printed and was followed in French, English, and German.

In the Council were delegates from 161 churches in 48 countries, representing some 160 million Christians (among the exceptions were the Roman Catholics), and many consultants and accredited visitors. The aims of this ecumenical gathering were to exchange views of the "continuing issues of Christian faith; to worship together; and to make policies and formulate programs for common association." The main theme was "Christ—The Hope of the World."

Bishop Oxnam is one of the outstanding speakers of the American Protestant clergy. He has tremendous force in delivery and strong intellectual and emotional drive. His Evanston sermon reflected his religious philosophy. He believes in the evangelical recognition of Christ as central in salvation, and in salvation as stressing social justice. He stresses Christ's help in the here and now as contrasted with the more orthodox eschatologists with their greater interest in the future life and Christ's Second Coming.

Bishop Oxnam attracted nation-wide attention by his statement before the House Committee on Un-American Activities, July 21, 1953. For nine hours the Bishop defended his record as an anti-Communist. The Committee was in complete agreement that the charges that Dr. Bromley

---

[1] By permission of Bishop G. Bromley Oxnam. The text is from *Current Religious Thought*. 14:1-9. July-August 1954. Because of the length of this address, a section only is included here. Students are advised to read the address in full.

[2] For biographical note, see Appendix.

Oxnam had been "soft on communism" had been without foundation. The Bishop also criticized sharply certain committee practices, for example, its making public of unverified and unevaluated evidence. His nine hours' appearance on that day was a striking demonstration of his extempore speaking and persuasive skill.

Six years have passed since we constituted a "fellowship of churches which accept our Lord Jesus Christ as God and Saviour." Within that fellowship, we have worshipped, witnessed, and worked together.

We intend to stay together.

We have learned how to study, to speak, to stand and to serve together. In humility but with firm resolve, we declare in Evanston as we did at Amsterdam, "We intend to stay together."

At Amsterdam, in solemn procession, we entered the Nieuwe Kerk. Together, we sang the Old Hundredth—"All people that on earth do dwell." It was sung in the French of Theodore Beza and in many other tongues. A representative of the Dutch Reformed Church read the Call to Worship and we heard him declare, "His Kingdom is forever." In that procession, some wore the gorgeous vestments of the Eastern Orthodox Churches and some the simple, significant uniform of the Salvation Army. Some were bareheaded; others wore velvet caps and birettas; and still others from the Malabar Coast wore the beautiful headdresses upon which were embroidered crosses that symbolized our Blessed Lord and the Twelve. Some wore the ruffled collars of Scandinavia; and some were clad in business suits. But we were one in Christ Jesus.

We intend to stay together.

It fell to me to preside over the committee charged with such mundane matters as budgets, financial organization, and staffing. Strangely enough, these meetings proved to be an unforgettable spiritual experience. At the close of each day we united in Evening Worship. The minister read, "God is a Spirit: and they that worship Him must worship in spirit and truth." Together, we repeated the Apostles' Creed. As the service concluded, the minister said, "Into Thy hands, O Lord,

I commend my spirit" and we responded together, "For Thou hast redeemed us, O Lord, Thou God of truth."

We intend to stay together.

These devotional services were led by John Baillie, Scotsman and Presbyterian; by Father Florovsky, Russian and Orthodox; by Hans Lilje, German and Lutheran; and by Henry Knox Sherrill, American and Protestant Episcopalian. When we bowed in prayer, I was unaware of the fact that my brother was Scotch or Russian or German or American; I did not think of the communion he represented; I knew we were brothers, united in love, loyal to our Blessed Lord, children of one Father. We were together.

We intend to stay together. . . .

Is there a more compelling obligation placed upon clergy and laity alike than to discover the concrete means by which the ethical ideals of religion may be translated into the realities of the common life? Perhaps there is no greater need among us, assuming the faith, than for competent laymen who within the realm of their competency will discover the means by which the faith may live in world law and order, economic justice and racial brotherhood. It is thus that socially necessary service becomes spiritually significant and vocation becomes sacred.

When competent Christians seek to express the worth of personality in political institutions they speak of "government of the people, by the people, and for the people." They declare that "all men are created equal and endowed with certain unalienable rights." They insist that "government derives its just powers from the consent of the governed." They hold that their institutions shall be conceived in liberty. Thus they affirm that the state does not confer our liberties, it merely confirms them. They belong to us because we are men, because we are sons of God. We are endowed with these rights. They cannot be alienated. . . .

I do not accept the criticism that the Church has lost touch with dominant realities; but I do agree that we who believe we are co-workers with the Eternal Himself and who hold that Christ is ever with us, could have been far more effective than we have been in establishing the conditions of justice in the name of One who said, "A new commandment give I unto you, that ye love one another."

Since we are meeting upon American soil, I am sure that delegates from overseas and from other nations of the Western Hemisphere will pardon me when I point out certain evidences of very close touch with dominant realities. It was in 1908 that the Social Creed of the Churches was drafted. Its first statement reads, "The Churches stand for equal rights and complete justice for all men in all stations of life." I have never liked the terms "the individual Gospel" and "the social Gospel." There is one Gospel, a whole Gospel with its message of redemption for the individual and for society. The Gospel eventuates in the changed individual, in the new man in Christ Jesus. It also eventuates in the changed society, not only in a new heaven but in a new earth.

It is but to state the fact to declare that the practices of American business in 1954 differ so fundamentally from the practices of 1900 that the same term cannot be used to describe them. This amazing change has been wrought in large measure because of the prophetic proclamation of the Christian faith and the clear statement of its demand for justice. Responsible leaders in business and in labor, pledged to the moral principles that lie at the heart of the Christian faith, regard themselves as men upon whom heavy obligation has been placed. A man who would corner the wheat market today would not be called a genius. On the contrary, he would be called a gangster. It was but yesterday that one of the most distinguished bishops of my own Church was castigated as subversive because he had served as chairman of a commission that had investigated the steel strike of 1919. At that time, men worked twelve hours a day in steel and seven days a wek. On the change of shift, they were often ordered to work twenty-four consecutive hours. The bishop and his associates were called upon to preach the "simple" gospel, to concern themselves with spiritual matters. I do not know of a responsible business leader in the nation today who would think of advocating a twelve-hour day in any industry, nor a seven-day week. We have moved on. We have been in touch with dominant realities.

Yesterday, child labor was a fact.

> No fledgling feeds the father bird,
> No chicken feeds the hen:
> No kitten mouses for the cat;
> That glory is for men.
>
> We are the wisest, strongest race,
> Loud may our praise be sung,
> The only animal alive
> That lives upon its young.

Child labor! The Church has been in touch with reality, and child labor in this land is a thing of the past. There were those among us who insisted that such discussions were without the realm of the Church's proper interest. They did not understand Berdyaev's dictum: Bread for me is a materialistic matter; but bread for my brother is a spiritual matter.

There were many who in the name of religion revealed they were unacquainted with the obligations of religion. They had failed to read the Magnificat of Mary. They had forgotten, if they had ever known, the sermon Jesus preached at Nazareth. The clearcut speech of the twenty-third chapter of Matthew had escaped their attention. There are still some among us who would have us silent upon the issue of justice. They are an irritating minority and the more vocal among them are but lonely voices upon a deserted battlefield. The army has marched on. Christian leaders are determined to work together for justice.

We intend to stay together.

It must be made clear that we dare not identify the Gospel of Jesus with any historically conditioned political, social or economic system. The Gospel stands in judgment upon all of them. Some, unacquainted with the Gospel, seek to judge the Gospel itself by the prevailing mode of production, by the particularly political system under which they live and by the social practices of their particular community. Christians, on the contrary, judge all economic systems by the imperatives of the Christian faith. The Christian Gospel is not to be found in Adam Smith's *Wealth of Nations* nor in Karl Marx's *Das Kapital*. It is to be found in Matthew, Mark, Luke and John, in the Acts of the Apostles, the Epistles of the New Testament and in the vision of John in the Revelation. It is to be found in the Hebrew prophets, in the lives of saints and martyrs, in the service of the faithful followers of Christ and in the continued revelation of God.

Christians who approach these complex and baffling problems will do well to kneel in devotion before they rise for discussion. Men who bow in repentant spirit at the table of the Lord make themselves ready to confer with brothers in the spirit of the Lord. The Communion Table should precede the conference table because conference with our fellows will be more productive when preceded by Communion with our Christ.

We intend to stay together.

Christians acquainted with the centuries know that the struggle to emancipate the worker is part of the age-long resolve to lift man to the status of brother. We hold that nothing can separate us from the love of God and therefore demand practices that express the love of God in service to our brothers. Thus we insist that the necessities of technology and the necessities of brotherhood be reconciled.

It is a matter of spiritual concern that the per capita annual income of China is $23; that the per capita annual income of India is $43; that the per capita annual income of Great Britain is $660; that the per capita annual income of the United States of America is $1500. These disparities in income are reflected in disparities in living standards. Brothers must face these facts together. There are 80 million cases of malaria in India today. One million die from malaria every year. Yet we know that the distinguished Minister of Health in India, a Christian and a woman, has pointed out—and the Rockefeller Foundation confirms—that for $23 million to buy jeeps, DDT, and spraying equipment, matched by $23 million of Indian labor and service, we can eradicate malaria from India in four years. These are spiritual issues, because justice for our brothers is a spiritual problem. Mr. Maurice Pate, head of UNICEF, United Nations International Children's Emergency Fund, recently addressed the Council of Bishops of my Church. Dealing with child life, he told of a disease popularly known as "yaws." A child stricken by yaws is crippled for life. Mr. Pate, a distinguished business-man, poignantly added, "For 15 cents it is possible to buy the penicillin necessary to cure a child suffering from yaws but there are vast areas of the earth where family income is so low that a father cannot provide the 15 cents with which to save his child." The World Council of Churches has spoken on such issues and will speak.

We intend to stay together.

It is well-nigh blasphemy to talk about the love of God and to declare that such issues are not the concern of the sons of God. In an hour when millions are being added to our Church rolls in one of the most significant evangelistic advances in the history of the Church, men and women who kneel at our altars must leave their gifts and go out to become right with their brothers. This we do that Christ's love may become regnant among men.

We must make it plain that the Christian demand for justice does not come from Karl Marx. It comes from Jesus Christ and the Hebrew prophets. We must bear in as good spirit as we can the stupidities of some current criticism. How can men know the Gospel unless they study the Gospel? There are some among us who will soon declare that Moses must have studied Marx. Did he not stand before an Egyptian king and demand "Let my people go"? Amos must have read the Communist Manifesto. Did he not cry out "Ye have sold the needy for a pair of shoes"? And some will irreverently suggest that our Lord was subversive. Did He not talk of those who devour widows' houses?

Upon these issues of freedom and of justice, we intend to stand together. We are children of a God of love. We are brothers.

We intend to stay together. . . .

We work in harmony with the moral law written into the nature of things. The universe is with us. Little dictators who strut the stage for a brief moment, who refuse to repeat the lines of the Eternal Playwright, who disregard the Divine Director, whose brazen voices shout immoral platitudes and obsolescent phrases, are doomed; the house empties, the footlights flicker, and upon a great backdrop are the words "Thou art weighed in the balances and found wanting." The universe was not made for madmen. It was not created for the lie.

The stage will be filled again. The players are those who have knelt at the feet of Christ. They stand to declare, "Thou art the Way, the Truth, and the Life." They have experienced His redeeming love. Under the compulsion of "Inasmuch as ye have done it unto one of the least of these My brethren, ye have done it unto Me" and in obedience to His command "Go ye into all the world and teach the nations to observe whatsoever things I have commanded you, baptizing them in the name of the Father and of the Son and of the Holy Spirit," they have played their parts. The stage is filled with blinding light, and a great chorus sings "O for a thousand tongues to sing my Great Redeemer's praise" and out of the light a voice is heard, "Ye have glorified Me upon the earth, ye have finished the work I gave you to do."

We intend to stay together.

Nothing can separate us from the love of God. Let the Redeemed of the Lord say so. Jesus Christ is to become the Ruler of the kings of the earth, King of Kings and Lord of Lords.

In this faith, *we intend to stay together.*

HOW TO HAVE GOOD RELATIONS
WITH OTHER PEOPLE [3]

Norman Vincent Peale [4]

The Reverend Norman Vincent Peale delivered this sermon at the Marble Collegiate Church, New York City, on October 18, 1953. The text below is a recorded transcription of the sermon as delivered extemporaneously.

Since 1932 Dr. Peale has been the dynamic pastor and preacher at the Marble Collegiate Church, Fifth Avenue, the oldest chartered church in New York City (founded in 1696). Each Sunday some four thousand see and hear him in person, with an overflow audience attending a closed-circuit TV service in the basement. In addition he has been broadcasting a weekly talk, "The Art of Living," over the National Broadcasting Network, to some one million homes, and he does a religious TV broadcast with his wife, "What's Your Trouble?" to some one hundred stations. His *Power of Positive Thinking,* based upon his sermons, led the list of non-fiction best sellers in 1953, 1954, and is in the lead in 1955. He now ranks, with Fulton J. Sheen, John Bonnell, and Ralph Sockman, as among the best known and most popular living American preachers.

Dr. Peale in sermonizing avoids theological complexities. He constantly deals with the immediate world. He sometimes analyzes public affairs and has taken a stand on such issues as support of the United Nations, labor interests, and condemnation of communism. He has been accused of injecting party politics into his public thinking. Basically, however, he concentrates on the individual and his religious problems. He has helped run a free religio-psychiatric clinic at his church. And into his sermonizing he has carried this same individual counseling. He uses such themes as "Believe in yourself," and "How to pray about your problems."

Dr. Peale's delivery is vigorous but conversational. He is free from undue "ministerial tones." His sermonic composition is simple, uncomplicated. His sentences and language are adjusted to the comprehension of millions. He fills his talks with his personal experiences, with direct dialogue, anecdotes, and with a background of biblical reference. He uses a text but is not interested in exegesis.

[3] Copyright, 1954, by Sermon Publications, Inc., Pawling, New York. Permission for this reprint through the courtesy of Dr. Norman Vincent Peale and of Sermon Publications.

[4] For biographical note, see Appendix.

This extremely active clergyman has been not only a prolific preacher, writer, and broadcaster, but also a popular speaker before businessmen's groups. In businesslike fashion he applies the current "how to do it" formula, to Christian living. The Sales Executives Club of New York described him as "America's most salesminded clergyman." He has well used the press, radio, and television to establish his religious speaking leadership in this age of mass communication.

Recently it was my privilege to address the student body of a university. Such an audience is, perhaps, the most demanding to which anyone can speak but it also offers a great opportunity. I consulted with a half dozen students and was advised that, while many speakers had dealt with world affairs and contemporary sociological interests, the students would also like to know how to live with the problems of daily life. I asked them to be specific and they said they wanted guidance on two problems: how to live without pressure, and how to get along with people. One sophomore confessed to feeling alone and rejected. He said he didn't get along with his parents, his professors, his associates. "There is something within myself," he said, "that makes it impossible for me to have happy personal relations. And I want relief."

This brought to my mind other people who have told me of having the same problem. I remember one very wealthy woman who had everything in a material sense to give her a satisfying life. She had a beautiful home and entertained lavishly, but she complained, "People come to my parties but they don't invite me to theirs." There was some quality about her that created a barrier between herself and others.

The personnel manager of a company told me that in his judgment the reason people fail in life is not so much a lack of ability or training, but simply that they never learn to have satisfactory relationships with people.

And so I am going to discuss this question with you. The person who is deficient in personal relations is inadequate; he hasn't been raised to his full potential, his full stature. What is the solution? Listen to this verse from the Book of Job: "If thou return to the Almighty thou shalt be built up." That is to say, get near to God; get your heart, your mind, your spirit filled with Jesus Christ and His attitudes. He will build you up to your full stature so that your relationships with other people will be happy and satisfactory.

How does this work itself out, practically? I always believe in making religion applicable, in a practical sense, to the problems of everyday life. When you return to the Almighty, you develop the ability to regard people with love and respect. There has been a great deal of emphasis placed upon *loving* other people. The Bible dwells on this in season and out. But not so much is said about *respecting* people. It is possible to have a sentimental attitude toward another person and at the same time not have high esteem for him.

The human personality demands love and it also demands respect. The great psychiatrist, Freud, says "Unless the personality has love, it sickens and dies." So if you give love to another human being you also give him health. He doesn't sicken; he gets well, because love is creative. Therefore the more love you give people, the healthier, happier, more vital you make them. Consequently they will love you; love will flow back to you. Of course, you cannot hold the good will of anybody if you wound his ego. Every human being has an inner sense of worth, of importance, of dignity. Wound that and you have lost that person forever. So when you love and respect a person you build him up and, accordingly, he loves and esteems you.

At one time I was on a program with an entertainer. I did not know the man well, but since that meeting I have noticed that he has been having difficulty and I think I know why.

I had been sitting beside him quietly for I was about to speak.

"You aren't nervous, are you?" he said.

"Why yes," I replied. "I always get a little nervous before I stand up before an audience. I have a profound respect for an audience and the responsibility makes me a bit nervous. Don't you get nervous?"

"No," he said. "Why should I? Audiences fall for anything. They are a lot of dopes."

"I don't agree with you," I said. "They are your sovereign judges. I have great respect for audiences." This man sent out no love to people and the reaction from the audience, while friendly, had a lack.

Later on I met an actor who told me that at one time he had the same attitude toward an audience. Then he began to get into difficulties; he wasn't being cast in important roles as he once had. A preacher gave him the suggestion that before going on stage, he pray for his audience; that he deliberately practice love and respect for them. So he stood in the wings at every performance and looked the audience over. He would pick out faces here and there and send out love-vibrations to them. He said that his rise in his profession dated from the time he learned to love and respect people.

You, too, have your audience every time you are in the presence of another human being. If you treat him with respect, he will entertain the same feeling for you. He may be a very simple, humble person, or one with great deficiencies. But if you are not "cocky"—to use a slang expression—or self centered, your good will and esteem will transmit itself to him.

Some people don't like others because they differ in religion, or live in another section of town, or are of another race. A person must be regarded for what he is, himself, and why shouldn't you esteem him? He is a child of God; Almighty God has breathed into him the breath of life. He is the finest mechanism ever made by the greatest of all artists; he has a divine origin, an immortal destiny and you owe him respect and love. For, of all factors in this world, a human being—any human being—is the greatest.

I have tested this law of the power of such thoughts or actual vibrations of power and I know it works. Sometime ago I went back to Ohio Wesleyan, the college where I graduated and where my daughter is now a student. Home-coming day is a big event there, and my daughter wrote that she wanted me to come and celebrate the day with her. A letter from her to me is a command. She wanted me to go with her to the football game.

I don't like to be away from New York on Saturday, but what could I do? I went to Ohio. I hired one of those "Drive-It-Yourself" cars because I didn't want to depend on anybody to get me to the Columbus airport after the game. I was late starting from Delaware, Ohio, where the college is located, and said to a friend, "I understand it is only twenty-five miles; I can get there easily in forty minutes, can't I?"

"It will take you an hour and a half," he said.

But I didn't have an hour and a half. I had an hour and fifteen minutes. So he outlined for me an alternate route whereby I could avoid the city of Columbus and its traffic. I had a vague knowledge of these roads, dating back thirty years. But many of them had changed. I never drive over fifty miles an hour except on an occasion. But this was an occasion! Anyway, I came to a turn, there was some loose gravel, and another car ahead. I had to jam on my brakes and the gravel shot over and hit that car like the ring of bullets. The driver turned and gave me a look that I can still see. It breathed venom and for the next three or four miles he deliberately prevented me from passing him.

Now I simply had to catch this plane from Columbus and the old Adam began to rise in me. I started to send out thoughts in this man's direction and you certainly wouldn't call them love-thoughts. Suddenly the thought came to me, "Why don't you practice what you preach? Relax, stop this mad rush. You don't have to catch this plane. There is another one in two hours. It gets in late, but you can take it." So I began to reason with myself, and to relax.

Finally I said to myself, "Why not practice the principle that you can get on better terms with this driver, who is annoyed, by sending out a vibration toward him—thoughts of good will and esteem." So I started saying, "The man in that car ahead is a child of God; he is a marvelous person. I will venture if we could stop and have dinner together, I would find him a wonderful fellow."

As I said this, naturally, I began to drive more moderately. And so did he, I continued to bombard the back of his head with love-thoughts and esteem. Then he must have noticed in his mirror that I was looking for the crossroad I had been told to take, and he put out his hand and motioned for me to drive up beside him.

"What are you looking for, Brother?" he said with a grin.

"The road to the airport," I answered. "I have to catch a plane and I'm late."

"Follow me," he said. "I'll take you there."

When we were almost at the airport he waved me on. I am sorry I do not know that man's name. When he drove away, with a smile on his face, I knew that I would love to have him for a friend. He is a nice fellow.

There is a sensitivity about human beings. Indeed, there is a sensitivity about animals. We have a cat at our house. I have always liked dogs but I never thought much of cats. But this is a wonderful cat; and this cat likes me, too. It is the smartest cat you ever saw. It has big, round eyes; and it got up on my desk the other day and settled down among my papers as if it wanted to be near me. Yes, sir, between that cat and myself there is affection because I have been sending out vibrations to it. The same is true of dogs. If you don't like a dog, he will react toward you indifferently, if not ferociously. Now, if this happens with dumb animals, certainly it must in the case of the highly-organized man. His subconscious, the essence of his personality, must react to the vibrations that go out from you to him. So get all hate out of your heart, all resentment, all ill will. Fill your heart with love and esteem for every individual, no matter how humble or irascible. Send such thoughts in his direction and you will, in turn, get his good will and cooperation.

What does that mean? Return to the way God does things, and you will have something to give people, something in yourself so creative, so dynamic, so worth-while that everyone will draw something from you. Thus they will like you and you will have good relations with people. Study the people you know who are the most beloved. They are the ones who have illimitable force and power. Anyone can be this way. Get close to Jesus Christ until your whole personality becomes saturated with Him.

I was talking to a man the other day about a doctor who was a friend of ours, one of the most glorious men I have ever known.

This man said, "If I could be sure Old Doc would be by my bedside when I die, so that I was looking on his face as I closed my eyes in death, I would be willing to die and I would have no fear."

And do you know, when I think of that doctor, I feel the same way about him. He is one of those men, like a great father, whom you snuggle up to in your weakness and sickness. He sends out love and faith to you.

I know the foreman in a factory whom people tell me they like to be around. As one man expressed it, "When I am with him I feel strong."

"How do you feel strong?" I asked.

"He seems to transmit strength to me," was the answer.

It is pathetic when we go through life living superficially, when there is no depth of meaning to our lives.

The reason many people do not get along, husbands with wives, business associates with each other, is simply because they do not have enough in themselves to give. Their associates find them empty. People who have something to give that is uplifting and helpful will always have people to love them.

A couple can transform the life of a community by having something to give. Let me tell you about such a couple with whom I had breakfast the other morning. They asked about fifteen other couples, as nice people as could be, to join us. The hosts called this breakfast meeting in order to do some spiritual sharing. They wanted to talk with their friends about Jesus Christ. "But," they said, "we have to do it in the right way. We want you to help us."

"I don't want to preach to them," I said. "That won't be effective."

"Just start talking to them," they told me.

So I started talking. I didn't have to talk very long before all of them were talking. And the whole conversation became sparkling, spiritual. All were busy people, but nobody wanted to leave. It got to be 10 A.M., and we were still sitting there, talking about Jesus Christ, about the way God helps people in their lives.

"Aren't these people wonderful!" I heard one man say to another. "I have been to a lot of social parties with these same people, but I never really knew them before. This meeting is far ahead of any I have ever had with them."

The reason we felt that way was that my friends were talking about things that build people up, that give them more faith, that make them feel stronger and better. No wonder everyone loved that couple.

Every human being, no matter how seemingly unattractive his personal composition may be, can make himself dynamic, fascinating and lovable. You and I, with all our deficiencies, are God's creation and He doesn't want us to be dull, negative, unattractive.

"If thou return to the Almighty, thou shalt be built up." God will restore your charm, the dynamic power of your personality, restore your vibrancy, fill your life with joy, love, and respect. These factors constitute the law of successful personal relations. Love people, respect them, and have something in you to give them. Return unto the Almighty who made you; and He will remake you.

CHRIST—THE HOPE OF THE WORLD [5]

ROBERT L. CALHOUN [6]

Dr. Robert L. Calhoun, professor of theology at Yale, gave this address at the first plenary session of the World Council of Churches, in McGaw Memorial Hall, Evanston, Illinois, on Sunday afternoon, August 15, 1954, on the Council theme, "Christ—The Hope of the World." The huge field house (McGaw Hall) was acoustically defective, the day was extremely hot, and the loudspeakers failed to operate efficiently.

The opening speaker of this first session was Dr. Edmund Schlink, a Lutheran and professor of dogmatic theology at Heidelberg University. He spoke in German and ran far overtime.

Dr. Calhoun's address, given before a depleted audience, was philosophically well reasoned. His style was hardly adjusted to the restless American delegates on that hot afternoon. The speaker interpreted the Council's theme and replied directly to Dr. Schlink's more conservative view of Christian eschatology.

Dr. Calhoun (who was a student of public speaking at Carleton College under I. M. Cochran, a celebrated teacher of debate) is effective on the platform, in ideas, language, and delivery. He has been in wide demand as a university speaker.

When a small company of men and women from a dozen countries, of widely diverse theological training and churchly tradition, work together for three years on a single theme, they learn much from one another. Their differences find some measure of reconciliation without ceasing to be real and important. Their words acquire new depth and clarity in face-to-face conversation. The theme itself becomes for them a living reality in which they share, a source of light that helps each to see himself and his companions with new insight. Hard-won mutual confidence takes the place of insecurity and mistrust. Disagreements are turned into common problems, not walls of separation.

But when the members of such a company try in a single week to share what they have found with thousands of fellow

[5] The text is from *Christian Century*. 71:1005+. August 25, 1954. By permission of *Christian Century*, and through the courtesy of Professor Robert L. Calhoun.

[6] For biographical note, see Appendix.

Christians even more diverse in experience, unprepared by close companionship and quiet conversation, the results are hard to predict. Under such conditions it is needful that we talk frankly to one another not only about our theme, but also about ourselves in relation to it. Christian life and thought in any of our countries is far too complex and diverse to be written off in a few simple formulas. There has been far too much premature judgment both of our theme and of one another, in spoken and in printed words. One part of our task here is to clear away some of these false and one-sided preconceptions. Our concern is not to obscure or to obliterate differences but to set them in clearer, truer light, so that each of us may learn from his neighbors, and our differences, purged of arrogance and error, may come to enrich, not to violate, the unity we affirm.

I

Our theme, as all the world knows by this time, requires that we seek some common understanding of Christian eschatology. This is by no means the whole meaning of the theme, but it defines an essential perspective in which the meaning must be interpreted. The eschatological perspective, however, is itself at times a subject for debate and a source of division. Such debate has occurred repeatedly in Christian history, and it is not unfamiliar to those who have helped prepare for this assembly.

The difficulty is not merely that the word "eschatology" is a somewhat formidable one, less familiar in some parts of the church than in others. It would be frivolous and unforgivable to let any word, merely because it is large or strange, block the road to common understanding. The real trouble has been that the word "eschatalogy" is all too easily misinterpreted by omitting or underemphasizing essential aspects of its meaning. The ordinary popular paraphrase, "doctrine of the last things," actually favors such misinterpretation. It suggests much too simply either some "far-off divine event" at the end of a long, vague future, without direct bearing on our life today; or else an end of the world at a particular date, calculated by methods for which most of us find no good warrant in either Scripture or Christian experience, and in which most of us do not believe.

Preoccupation with "the end" as if it were a date on the calendar—the final date, the only crucial one that still awaits us —and neglect of "the present" as comparatively trivial in importance leads to one sort of distortion. Preoccupation with "the present" and refusal to take seriously the significance of "the end," in its biblical and Christian sense, leads to another sort. Both these errors are made easier when we oversimplify the admittedly difficult concept of Christian eschatology into a static "doctrine of the last things."

Happily, there is a better reading of the word, closer both to the classical and to the biblical meaning of its component parts. Eschatology is the doctrine concerned with *the limits or boundaries* of our living, in time and existence, toward which at every moment our whole lives tend.

For Christian faith, God revealed in Jesus Christ is the boundary of our time and our existence, at once infinitely beyond us and immediately near. For us He who is our Creator, the First, of our being, is at the same time the Last, the End that gives it significance. Time is our name for one order of the living relationships in which His presence and His acts are known to us and bear upon our lives. Time thus understood is neither illusory nor merely abstract or ideal. It is as concrete and actual as anything in the physical world. But it has no independent reality apart from the living God, Creator and Sustainer of the world, who makes Himself known in Jesus Christ as Redeemer, who as Holy Spirit acts unceasingly in human affairs.

Past, present and future are not separable segments of an endlessly outstretched line, a kind of space to be filled, but dimensions and directions within the living interaction of God and men. The future is not a kind of inverted past, nor an endless repetition of "tomorrows," but the homing of our unfinished lives to the One who gives them direction, meaning and fundamental security. He is the One who comes to meet us at every moment, yet who lives and promises that we can live beyond the limits of earthly time and space. Hope is then not a mere expectation of things wished for, but the powerful, deep impulse with which we face joyfully and confidently toward the living boundary, the true end of our lives and of our world, at once here-now and yet-to-be. This is to say, in the profounder language that runs in a great crescendo throughout the Bible, God himself—"the God who said, 'Let light shine out of darkness,' who has shone in our hearts to give the light of the knowledge of the glory of God in the face of Jesus Christ," God the Father, Son and Holy Spirit—He is our hope, who enables us so to live.

To think of eschatology in these terms is to reaffirm with full vigor the basic insights of a theology that finds the Kingdom of God, the lordship of Jesus Christ and the power of the Holy Spirit very present living reality. The Kingdom of God is of all present realities the most real, the providential order full of vital tensions, the cleansing flame of judgment and the stillness of grace, the steady swell of sustaining power and the incessant denial of rest here, that gives meaning to our life on earth. The Lord Jesus Christ and the Holy Spirit are at work now with the incalculable power of truth and love, transforming both church and world. But the Kingdom and the Power are not restricted to the earthly doings of men. They work in judgment and mercy toward such glory for both church and world as we can neither foresee nor achieve. In all this is our hope, despite all the forces of evil here or hereafter.

In contrast to any simpler doctrine, Christian eschatology is multidimensional, paradoxical and dynamic. It is many-dimensional in the sense that, like good poetry or great music, it subjects us to the impact of reality at many levels, under many aspects, from many angles of approach; it demands of us readiness to respond in complex and subtle rather than in literal-minded, mechanical ways. Such complex response need not be sophisticated and technically expert, still less bookish or pedantic. But it must be imaginative and discerning, with the many-faceted vision of the childlike mind that Jesus praised—the mind unfettered by prematurely rigid notions of time and space, of nature and man, and therefore able to see the "eternal power and deity" of God in and through "the things that have been made," the impending fulfillment of His Kingdom foreshadowed in the events of everyday.

The doctrine is paradoxical (or dialectical) in the sense that in trying to suggest the profound, mysterious truth of our lives in a world sustained and negated, transformed and fulfilled, drawn forward and everywhere met by the living presence of God, it combines contrary affirmations that have to be affirmed together and that lose their meaning if they are separated. This is not contradiction. A self-contradictory utterance tries to combine factors that may be quite intelligible taken separately but make nonsense when combined. Square triangles, uncreated creatures, unthinking intellects are contradictions, nonsense terms that refer to nothing real. But when Jesus says, "He that loses his life shall find it," or when Paul writes, "It is no longer I that live, but Christ liveth in me," or "We preach a Messiah crucified, . . . God's power and God's wisdom," these are not contradictions. They speak paradoxically of reality too vital and profound to be analyzed or fully defined.

So it is when we hear of the Kingdom that is already "in the midst" of Jesus' listeners and yet is still to come "as a thief in the night," or of Paul's life "in the Spirit" now, which at the same time presses on to a goal not yet attained. This is the language of paradox that we use without hesitation when we try to understand the mysteries of love, loyalty and self-sacrifice, of individual and social existence, of human bondage and human freedom. It should not surprise us that such language is needed when we try to think about the Kingdom of God.

This doctrine is dynamic in the sense that it sees the end that is yet to be as already at work giving direction and meaning to what now is. It sees the present as full of both past and future —not flatly identical with them, but full of tensions both life-giving and destructive, because it participates in what has been and what is yet to be. Past, present and future are not segments of a line that stand outside one another. Neither are they merely three names for one single fact. They are inseparable and interpenetrating dimensions of life, in which men and God meet one another in the fluid counterpoint of living communication. Memory, realization and hope likewise are not three words with one meaning. Neither do they stand for three independent realities or responses. They are inseparable, interpenetrating, active attitudes of men who face God and one another in the living web of time and history.

The fundamental reality is God, His Kingdom and His righteousness, ever present and ever coming to judge and to bless His creatures. He is our hope, because in Jesus Christ He has come down into the midst of earthly history, taken our cross upon His shoulders and our wounds into His heart, met death and hell face to face for our sake, and filled the human scene with a vast new light in which we men are judged and blessed as never before. He is our hope because in Jesus Christ, died and risen, He gives us promise of strength to endure the stress of earthly battle, and of life with Him beyond all earthly bounds.

On some such understanding of Christian eschatalogy and of our hope in Jesus Christ the members of the Advisory Commission have agreed.

II

But very difficult problems remain, for our discussions here and for our life and thought as fellow Christians when we return to our homes. Even those who agree on a provisional statement of belief are sure to understand it diversely, and to others it may be quite unacceptable.

The reason, of course, is that each of us is conditioned in all sorts of ways, conscious and unconscious, by his own unique place in the fluid network of history. Each shares with his nearest neighbors—though never completely even with them—a great body of cultural and churchly tradition, of practical attitudes and presuppositions, of memories, loyalties and hopes. To each his understanding of the gospel has been mediated, in large measure, through these living historical involvements. For each, therefore, not the whole gospel as God knows it but some aspect or version of the gospel as a man can know it—"in a mirror dimly"—is disclosed.

It is right that each shall affirm with conviction what his own "eyes have seen" and his "hands have touched, concerning the word of life." When such affirmation is guided by clear recognition of the finiteness of every man and every historical version of the gospel—not only those cherished in other countries or church traditions, but also one's own—then together we may be led by the Holy Spirit into more ample vision of the truth. But when we lack such critical self-knowledge and claim finality and completeness for our partial visions, forgetting that we all are "men and not God," then we risk turning the light in us into darkness. This is the reason that we must talk frankly together not only about our theme but also about ourselves.

Each of us can speak most helpfully about the people, the tradition and the way of understanding the gospel that he knows best, and so I shall speak here. Each of us, moreover, will know that he and his nearest neighbors cannot fairly be described in clichés. None of us is a walking stereotype: an activist or a pessimist, a liberal or a neo-orthodox thinker, a Continental or an American Christian. All of us know that to be content with pinning labels like these on one another is a confession of ignorance, not a sign of understanding.

At the same time, such labels can have a legitimate use. They can serve to remind us that though the gospel is one, our ways of reading it are many; that our varied perspectives are shaped by generations of varied living and deserve patient exploration together until we can recognize their proper meanings and their common source; that each needs the other for illumination and correction; and that, by God's grace, these human differences must find their true, vital place within a shared life vaster and more deeply united than any of us has yet known.

III

One such human perspective, shared by many Protestant Christians in North America and in other lands, is often labeled "American activism." The phrase is misleading, for "activism" has been a major factor in Christian life from the beginning, had a large place in the Reformation, and is strong today wherever Christians take responsible parts in public life. But for all that, the term does refer to a familiar American disposition—a source at once of real difficulties and of great potential strength, as yet but partly realized, for the church in our time. The men and women who in three hundred years have settled and brought to national status the United States and Canada have been, of necessity, very active and busy people. Most of their energies have been expended in taming a continent, building homes, towns and cities, establishing and maintaining popular government on a hitherto unprecedented scale, devising new techniques for controlling the forces of nature, and developing a vast system of education for more and more millions of children and youth. Today we, their sons and daughters, find ourselves called upon to play a new and difficult role in the active life of nations. The demand upon us is still mainly for deeds. We have perforce inherited and seek to practice, under God, the ways of self-reliant action; and when we think of hope, it is usually hope for a better life tomorrow, for our children, for the increasing number of those who depend on us and for whom we feel responsible.

In this context, much of our theology has come to lay especial stress on ethics and to be far less confident about eschatology. Two major roads have led to this result. One was frontier evangelism, the other the rise of the modern "social gospel." Until less than a hundred years ago the oldest Protestant churches in the New York maintained a vigorous, full-rounded theological tradition, mainly Calvinistic in temper, and produced theologians like Edwards and Bushnell who can stand with the ablest thinkers in Protestant history. But evangelists among the log cabins, in the forests and prairies and along the rivers of the inland frontier, had little use for theological subtlety. Their strength lay in devout, uncritical reading of the Bible, assurance of the presence of the Holy Spirit, and a rough and ready gospel for rough and busy men. They preached about heaven and hell, but their central concern was life here and now. Theirs was a homespun theology, remote from the college and seminary classrooms of the Atlantic seaboard.

Moreover, in the nation-building period since 1865, a time of swiftly accelerated growth of cities, industrialization, scientific and technical advance, and development of state-supported schools and universities that exclude dogmatic instruction, a major part of our academic Protestant theology itself came to be

concerned less with the structure of biblical and traditional doctrines and more with the task of redressing injustice in the new
industrial and political scene. This social and moral stress has a
solid foundation in the Reformed theology shared, in one form
or another, by most North American Protestants. It found support also in the moral and social interpretation of the gospel in
Ritschlian thought, which many of our biblical and theological
teachers studied in Germany and adapted to the American situation. For many reasons it seemed and still seems to many devoted American Christians the most relevant way of preaching
the gospel to a vast, diverse, hurrying society, widely convinced
of the positive values of the sciences and technology and the
present obligations of free men and women.

For such theology the Kingdom of God, the lordship of
Jesus Christ and the power of the Holy Spirit have had very
concrete, present and imperative meaning. Often too simply,
but in all sincerity, such theology has echoed the gospel word:
"The Kingdom of God is in the midst of you," and has taken
very seriously the reply to John the Baptist and the injunctions
about feeding the hungry and setting prisoners free. It has
found signs of the breaking in of God's Kingdom here at home
in the advancing conquest of diseases and hunger, the abolition
of chattel slavery and the extension of Christian conscience from
private to public affairs. Its hope has been centered in the manifest power of God to overcome evil with good here and now,
and throughout man's future on earth. It does not forget the
final judgment nor the life everlasting, but its chief confidence
has been in God's grace from day to day, and its chief stress on
the duty of every Christian to live as a devoted follower and
servant of Jesus Christ.

This theology is not irresponsible. It is not given to elaborate speculations, to emotional extravagance, nor to moral inaction. Neither is it divorced from either biblical or traditional
Christianity. It makes much of the prophetic teachings in the
Old Testament, the centrality of Jesus Christ in the Gospels,
and the summons to follow Him in obedience to His Father.
Moreover, it takes seriously in practice, without much theoretic
discussion, the traditional judgment that the Christian gospel is

a word for this world, a truly historical word rooted in actual existence and demanding present day-by-day response, not a remote ideal nor a way of escape. It affirms also, in strenuous if not always well directed action as well as in spoken and written language, the Reformers' insistence that this world must be transformed according to the will of God, our Creator and Redeemer. Its most characteristic prayer is, "Thy Kingdom come, Thy will be done on earth." Its characteristic hope looks for the ever-clearer manifestation of God's sovereignty and the power of his promises in human history.

As far as it goes, this is sound and basic Christian doctrine. But it is neither proof against distortions nor free from shortcomings. The most dangerous distortions spring from the group egotism that is universal among men, and that takes among us a distinctive cultural and theological form. We tend to confuse the will of God with our way of life, and to suppose that our version of the gospel of hope is the only one that is meaningful and true.

It is perilously easy for us to identify God's promises with the peculiarly American way of life; to suppose that the Kingdom of God is, at least in principle, our republican form of government, the economic system we call free enterprise, the social and cultural heritage we cherish. If all these assumptions were true, then the Kingdom of God would be established on earth precisely if and when our particular way of life was imposed on all peoples. To state such a position clearly is enough to make plain its un-Christian character. As Christians, we do not and cannot really believe anything of this sort. We may well cherish (without exaggerating) the measures of freedom, justice and simple decency in our heritage, and try to help others gain like benefits. We may well defend vigorously what is good in our national life when it is threatened. But the sharpest self-criticism is needed if we are to be thus loyal without turning the object of our loyalty into an idol, immune to criticism and jealous of any rival.

Further, like fellow Christians in every country and in every part of the church, we are apt to regard our own understanding of the gospel as, at least in principle, both correct and sufficient.

To maintain sturdily that we see and know in part the authentic gospel is one thing. To affirm that what we see and know is the whole truth, and to reject or disparage what others see in a different perspective from our own, is quite another. It will not do to claim for any particular doctrinal tradition or current habit the infallibility of God. We are all fellow servants, none of us entitled to lord it over the rest. Jesus spoke sharp words for those who call their brothers simpletons and fools. We Protestants of North America may properly hope that all our brothers will heed the Lord's admonition, but our first responsibility is to remember it as a word addressed directly to us.

This bears immediately on our treatment of the main theme in discussion here. In at least two familiar ways "American activism" can hamper, unless we are alert, our understanding of the gospel of hope. These limitations should not be exaggerated or misjudged, but they must not be ignored. First, there is always a tendency for moral earnestness to stiffen into dogmatic moralism that centers attention on human effort and thinks of Christian hope primarily as assurance that our best efforts will succeed, with God's help. It is surely right to keep our eyes on goals that seem to accord with God's will, and to work toward them with unflagging devotion and confidence. But it is seriously wrong to think of God primarily as one who guarantees the achievement of our cherished goals, or to judge the truth of His promises by the measure of our success. It is right to be assured that in His keeping our work is not in vain. Yet there is need to remind ourselves constantly that God's ways are not our ways nor His thoughts our thoughts; that Christ our hope was crucified before He was raised in glory; that God's will, not ours, is to be done.

A second limitation often regarded as typical of our thought is the supposition that the Kingdom will be fully realized within earthly history. Here again a valid insight is involved. This world is God's world. His Kingdom enfolds it and His will is being done in the midst of it, overcoming its evils with the redeeming power of good. But as recent events should remind us again, there is no sign that earthly history is being progressively purged of evil and steadily nearing perfection. On the contrary, new achievements bring new perils and new forms of corruption. As far ahead as we can see or think, vast forces of evil deeply rooted in the lives of persons and societies, taking unforeseeable new forms as the patterns of life change from generation to generation, beset the way at every stage. And death, "the last enemy," armed at this moment with terrible new weapons, waiting inexorably at every moment, stands across the path of every human person and people. Whatever can be achieved in earthly history—and no one but God can judge how great the achievement will be—a hope that can rightly triumph over such hydra-headed perils must envisage in some sense "a new heaven and a new earth."

Again it is God and not we who can know what this new order will be. Too confident speculation is out of place, and we American Protestants for the most part have sought to avoid it. But in so doing we have often lost touch with the faith of the church through the centuries, that in "the age to come" there will be a new corporate life in a new environment, in the full light of the presence of God.

IV

When the first Christians began to proclaim their good news that the God of heaven and earth was in Christ, crucified and risen, recalling the world to Himself, they were preaching to people harassed by fears and confused by false hopes. The Gentiles feared both man and nature, death and the mysterious powers of fate and fortune. The Roman talent for conquest and government had promised at least political security around the Mediterranean basin. But the republic of old Rome had gone down in a welter of civil wars, and given place to rule by a haphazard series of autocrats threatened by conspiracies at home and by barbarians inside and outside the empire. As for nature, fate and death, the Greek hope in reason, once held high in the great philosophic schools though never dominant in everyday life, was rapidly fading in a revival of skepticism and pious irrationalism.

Into that troubled world the preaching of the gospel brought a great surge of new hope. By the act of God in Jesus Christ,

Ignatius of Antioch wrote as the second century began, "all sorcery was dissolved and every chain of wickedness vanished away, ignorance was removed, and the old kingdom was destroyed; for God was manifest as man for the newness of eternal life, and that which had been prepared by God received its beginning."

Today the first part of that exultant word is still awaiting fulfillment. The gospel now has been preached on every continent, but most men—including us who proclaim it—have never really understood and lived by it. The church has now encircled the globe, but displays in its own life the anxious rivalries and inner conflicts of the world. Once more mankind is torn by wars and civil strife, not of armies only but of whole peoples. Once more forces of nature and feats of reason, that seemed for a time to be our more and more obedient servants, have put on—thanks to our own folly—the masks of destructive demons. Once more death stands at our elbow, unforgettable, and goes with us wherever we go.

The word of hope to such a world must still be the gospel on which the martyr bishop of Antioch staked his life: that the God of Hosts is with us, that in Jesus Christ He has come to share our lot and break the tyranny of sin and death, that therein "that which had been prepared by God received its beginning," and that the course of history and the end of all things are in His hand. That gospel on the lips of apostles and martyrs struck root in a hostile world. We are here today from the ends of the earth in witness to its power. If we in turn can proclaim it in language for our day, with something like their burning faith, we too shall find in Christ the hope of man.

APPENDIX

BIOGRAPHICAL NOTES

BREBNER, JOHN BARTLET (1895-   ). Born, Toronto, Canada; student, University of Toronto Schools, 1910-13; University of Toronto, 1913-15; B.A., St. John's College, Oxford University, 1920; M.A., B.Litt., Oxford University, 1925; Ph.D., Columbia University, 1927; Litt.D., Brown University, 1944; Lecturer in modern history, University of Toronto, 1921-25; instructor in history, Columbia University, 1925-27; assistant professor, 1927-35; associate professor, 1935-42; professor since 1942; served in Canadian Army, 1915-18, in British Army, 1918; fellow, Royal Geographical Society; member, historical societies and recipient of distinguished scholarships and appointments; author of *The Function of Graduate Studies,* 1945; contributor to magazines and encyclopedias.

BRICKER, JOHN WILLIAM (1893-   ). Born, Madison County, Ohio; A.B., Ohio State University, 1916, LL.B., 1920; admitted to Ohio bar, 1917; Assistant Attorney General of Ohio, 1923-27, Attorney General, 1933-37; Governor of Ohio, 1939-45; Republican candidate for vice president, 1944; United States Senator from Ohio since 1945; First Lieutenant, United States Army, World War I; member Delta Sigma Rho, Order of Coif, and other honorary and professional societies. (See also *Current Biography: 1943.*)

CALHOUN, ROBERT L. (1896-   ). Born, St. Cloud, Minnesota; B.A., Carleton College, 1915, LL.D., 1946; B.D., Yale University, 1918, M.A., 1919, Ph.D., 1923; D.D., University of Chicago, 1941, Oberlin College, 1944; instructor in philosophy, Carleton College, 1921-23; instructor in historical theology, Yale University, 1923-26, associate professor 1932-36, professor since 1936; special lecturer at Yale, Ohio Wesleyan, Pacific School of

Religion, Harvard, Vanderbilt, Chicago, and other universities; member Phi Beta Kappa, Delta Sigma Rho; author or co-author of books, including *Religion and the Modern World,* 1940.

DOUGLAS, PAUL H. (1892-   ). Born, Salem, Massachusetts; A.B., Bowdoin College, 1913; A.M., Columbia University, 1915, Ph.D., 1921; instructor in economics, University of Illinois, 1916-17; Reed College, 1917-18; associate professor of economics, University of Washington, 1919-20; successively assistant professor, associate professor, and professor of industrial relations, University of Chicago, 1920-1948; service on many commissions related to unemployment; Guggenheim fellowship, 1931; member Advisory Committee to United States Senate and Social Security Board, 1937; Private, later Major, in Marine Corps, 1942-45; wounded, battle of Okinawa; awarded Bronze Star for heroic service; elected United States Senator (Democrat) from Illinois, 1948, reelected in 1954; member, Phi Beta Kappa, and other learned societies; author of *Wages and the Family,* 1925; *Theory of Wages,* 1934; and some dozen other books. (See also *Current Biography: 1949.*)

DULLES, JOHN FOSTER (1888-   ). Born, Washington, D.C.; B.A., Princeton University, 1908, LL.D., 1946; Sorbonne, Paris, 1908-09; LL.B., George Washington University, 1911; LL.D., Tufts College, Wagner College, Northwestern University; began law practice, New York City, 1911; director, Bank of New York; trustee, Rockefeller Foundation; chairman, Carnegie Endowment for International Peace; chairman, Federal Council of Churches Commission on a Just and Durable Peace; secretary to a delegation, Hague Peace Conference, 1907; Captain and Major, United States Army, 1917-18; member, Reparations Commission and Supreme Economic Council, 1919; member, United States delegation, San Francisco Conference on World Organization, 1945; Council of Foreign Ministers, London, 1945; General Assembly, United Nations, 1946; meeting of Council of Foreign Ministers, Moscow, 1947; London meeting of "Big Four," 1947; appointed United States Senator (Republican) from New York, July-November 1949 (to complete term of

Senator Wagner); appointed counselor, Department of State, April 1950; appointed, with rank of ambassador, to negotiate terms of peace for Japan, 1951; representative at signing of Japanese peace treaty, San Francisco, 1951; writer and speaker on international affairs; author of *War or Peace,* 1950; appointed Secretary of State in the Eisenhower cabinet, 1953. (See also *Current Biography: 1953.*)

EISENHOWER, DWIGHT D. (1890-   ). Born, Denison, Texas; B.S., United States Military Academy, 1915; Army Tank School, 1921; graduate, War College, 1929; Second Lieutenant, United States Army, 1915; Lieutenant Colonel, Tank Corps, World War I; advanced through grades to General of the Army, December 1944; Chief of Operations Division, Office of Chief of Staff, 1942; Commanding General, European Theatre of Operations, June 1942; Allied Commander in Chief, North Africa, November 1942; Supreme Commander of Allied Land, Sea, and Air Forces in Western Europe, November 1943; Chief of Staff, United States Army, 1945-48; President of Columbia University, 1948-52; appointed Supreme Commander of the North Atlantic Treaty Nations, 1950; entered in presidential primaries on Republican ticket, January 1952; elected President of the United States, November 1952; author of *Crusade in Europe,* 1948, *Eisenhower Speaks,* 1948. (See also *Current Biography: 1948.*)

KNOWLAND, WILLIAM F. (1908-   ). Born, Alameda, California; A.B., University of California, 1929; publisher, Oakland *Tribune* since 1933; member, California State Assembly, 1933-35, Senate, 1935-39; United States Army, 1942-45; appointed to United States Senate and elected to full term, 1946; reelected 1952; Republican majority leader, United States Senate, 1952-54; minority leader, Eighty-fourth Congress, first session, 1955. (See also *Current Biography: 1947.*)

LIPPMANN, WALTER (1889-   ). Born, New York City; A.B., Harvard University, class of 1910 (degree taken, 1909), graduate student, 1909-10; associate editor, *New Republic,* and editor, New York *World;* after 1931 special writer for New York *Herald Tribune* and other newspapers; assistant to Secretary of War, 1917; Captain, United States Army Military Intelligence, A.E.F., 1917-18; member, Board of Overseers, Harvard University, 1933-39; writer of column, "Today and Tomorrow," in about 180 papers; member, Phi Beta Kappa; author, *A Preface to Politics,* 1913; *Liberty and the News,* 1920; *The Phantom Public,* 1925; *A Preface to Morals,* 1929; *The United States in World Affairs,* 1931; *Interpretations,* 1933-35; *The Good Society,* 1937; *The United States Foreign Policy,* 1943; *Isolation and Alliances,* 1952; and other books. (See also *Current Biography: 1940.*)

LODGE, HENRY CABOT, JR. (1902-   ). Born, Nahant, Massachusetts; grandson of the late Senator Henry Cabot Lodge; A.B., Harvard University, 1924; with the Boston *Evening Transcript,* 1923; New York *Herald Tribune,* 1924; member of the Massachusetts General Court, 1933-36; elected United States Senator (Republican) from Massachusetts, 1936, for the term ending 1943; on leave, Major, United States Army Tank Corps, with the British forces, 1942; Lieutenant-Colonel, southern France, Rhine, southern Germany, 1944-45; reelected to the Senate, 1946; defeated for reelection, 1952; appointed by President Eisenhower United States chief delegate to the United Nations, 1953. (See also *Current Biography: 1954.*)

MACARTHUR, DOUGLAS (1880-   ). Born, Arkansas; graduate, United States Military Academy, 1903; graduate, Engineer School of Application, 1908; D.Sc., Pennsylvania Military Academy, 1928; many other honorary degrees; Brigadier General, United States Army, 1918; Major General, 1925; General, 1930; served in Philippines, 1903-04, Japan, 1905-06; army service schools, 1910-12; in Vera Cruz Expedition, 1914; general staff, 1913-17; Commander of 42nd Division (Rainbow), 1918; Meuse-Argonne and other offensives; twice wounded in action; army of occupation in Germany, 1918-19; Chief of Staff, United States Army, 1930-35; Commander, United States armed forces in Far East, 1941-51; appointed Supreme Commander land, air, and sea forces, Southwest Pacific, 1942; decorated D.S.C., D.S.M., and awarded many other military honors; General of the Army, 1944; Supreme Commander occupational forces in Japan, 1945-51; Commander of United Nations forces, Korean War, 1950-51; dismissed by President Truman, April 1951; member, Board of Directors, Remington Rand, since 1952. (See also *Current Biography: 1948.*)

MURROW, EDWARD R. (1909-   ). Born, Greensboro, North Carolina; B.A., Washington State College, 1930; student, Stanford University and University of Washington; president, National Student Federation, 1930-32; assistant director, Institute of International Education, 1932-35; with Columbia Broadcasting System since 1935; chief of European service, 1937-46; vice president, Columbia Broadcasting System, 1945-47; now reporter and news analyst; daily news broadcasts and "This I Believe" and "Hear It Now" programs; "See It Now" television program since 1951, and "Person to Person" since 1953; many awards for his radio-television programs. (See also *Current Biography: 1953.*)

NIXON, RICHARD MILHOUS (1913-   ). Born, Yorba Linda, California; A.B., Whittier College, 1934; LL.B., Duke University Law School, 1937; general practice of law, Whittier, California, 1937-43; attorney with Office of Emergency Management, Washington, D.C., 1942; Lieutenant-Commander, United States Navy, 1942-46; member, House of Representatives (Republican, California), 1947-1950; Senate, 1951-52; elected Vice President of the United States on the Republican ticket, 1952. (See also *Current Biography: 1948.*)

OXNAM, G. (GARFIELD) BROMLEY (1891-   ). Born, Sonora, California; A.B., University of Southern California, 1913; S.T.B., Boston University, 1915, Litt.D., 1930; studied also in Japan, China, India, 1919; honorary degrees at College of the Pacific, Wesleyan, Ohio Wesleyan, Wabash, Yale, De Pauw, and other universities and colleges; California Methodist pastorates, 1916-27, including Church of All Nations, 1917-1927:

professor of practical theology and the city church, Boston University School of Theology, 1927-28; president, DePauw University, 1928-36; elected Bishop, Methodist Church 1936; Omaha area, 1936-39, Boston area, 1939-44, New York Area, 1944-1952; lecturer at theological schools and at many universities; president, Federal Council of Churches, 1944-46; one of the presidents of World Council of Churches. (See also *Current Biography: 1944.*)

PEALE, NORMAN VINCENT (1898-   ). Born, Bowersville, Ohio; graduate, Bellefontaine, Ohio, high school; A.B., Ohio Wesleyan University, 1920; S.T.B., M.A., Boston University, 1924; D.D., Syracuse University, 1931, Ohio Wesleyan University, 1936, Duke University, 1938; ordained ministry Methodist Episcopal Church, 1922; Kings Highway Methodist Episcopal Church, Brooklyn, 1924-27; University Methodist Episcopal Church, Syracuse, N.Y., 1927-32; Marble Collegiate Church, New York since 1932; editor since 1932, "Guideposts," inspirational magazine; recipient Freedom Foundation Award, 1952; author: *Art of Living,* 1937, *Guide to Confident Living,* 1948, *The Power of Positive Thinking,* 1952; writer for various secular and religious periodicals; speaker on various national radio programs, member of various commissions of Federal Council of Churches of Christ in America. (See also *Current Biography: 1946.*)

RANDALL, CLARENCE BELDEN (1891-   ). Born, Newark Valley, New York; student, Wyoming Seminary (Kingston, Pennsylvania) 1906-08; A.B., Harvard University, 1912, LL.B., 1915; LL.D., Northeastern University, 1948; law practice, Michigan, 1915-25; with Inland Steel since 1925; president since 1949; Captain, Infantry, United States Army, 1917-19; trustee, University of Chicago since 1936, Wellesley College, 1946-49; member, board of overseers, Harvard University since 1947; vice president, National Association of Manufacturers since 1946; chairman, President's Commission on Foreign Economic Policies, 1953-54; Phi Beta Kappa, Delta Upsilon; co-author, *Civil Liber-*

ties and Industrial Conflict, 1938; author, *Freedom's Faith,* 1953; contributor to magazines. (See also *Current Biography: 1952.*)

STENNIS, JOHN C. (1901-   ). Born, Kemper County, Mississippi; B.S., Mississippi State College, 1923; LL.B., University of Virginia, 1928; law practice, DeKalb, Mississippi; House of Representatives (Democrat, Mississippi), 1928-32; prosecuting attorney, 1931-35; Circuit Judge 1937-38, 1942, 1946; elected to United States Senate, 1946, reelected, 1952; member of Senate Committee to investigate charges against Senator Joseph McCarthy, 1954; member, Phi Beta Kappa and other honorary or professional societies. (See also *Current Biography: 1953.*)

STEVENSON, ADLAI EWING (1900-   ). Born, Los Angeles, California; A.B., Princeton University, 1922; J.D., Northwestern University Law School, 1926; LL.D., Illinois Wesleyan University, Northwestern University, Bradley University; reporter, *Daily Pantagraph* (Bloomington, Illinois), 1924-25; admitted to Illinois bar, 1926; member, Chicago law firms, 1927-41; assistant to Secretary of Navy, 1941-44; chief, Foreign Economic Administrations, Italy mission, 1943; assistant to Secretary of State, 1945; adviser, United States delegation, General Assembly of United Nations, London, 1946; United States delegate, General Assembly of United Nations, New York, 1946, 1947; governor of Illinois, 1948-52; Democratic candidate for president, 1952; tour around the world, 1953; author of *Speeches,* 1953, *Call to Greatness,* 1954. (See also *Current Biography: 1949.*)

CUMULATIVE AUTHOR INDEX

An author index to the volumes of *Representative American Speeches* for the years 1937-1938 through 1954-1955. The date following the title of each speech indicates the volume in which it appears.